Drunk Driving in America: Strategies and Approaches to Treatment

Drunk Driving in America: Strategies and Approaches to Treatment

Stephen K. Valle, Sc.D., C.A.C., F.A.C.A.T.A.
Editor

The Haworth Press
New York • London

Drunk Driving in America: Strategies and Approaches to Treatment has also been published
as *Alcoholism Treatment Quarterly*, Volume 3, Number 2, Summer 1986.

The Haworth Press, Inc., 12 West 32 Street, New York, NY 10001
EUROSPAN/Haworth, 3 Henrietta Street, WC2E 8LU England

Library of Congress Cataloging-in-Publication Data

Drunk driving in America.

Includes bibliographies.
1. Drunk driving—United States.   2. Drinking and traffic accidents—United States.
3. Alcoholism counseling—United States.   I. Valle, Stephen K.
HE5620.D7D78   1986   363.1′255′0973   86-18449
ISBN 0-86656-603-1

Drunk Driving in America: Strategies and Approaches to Treatment

Alcoholism Treatment Quarterly
Volume 3, Number 2

CONTENTS

Tess Kerns
Allen W. Gaskell

Contributors

Editor: Stephen K. Valle, Sc.D., C.A.C., F.A.C.A.T.A.
President, Valle Associates, Inc.
183 North Common Street, Lynn, MA 01905

George M. Appleton, Ph.D., N.C.C.
Director, Creative Interventions Alcohol Awareness Program
109 Faculty Office Building, State University College,
Brockport, New York 14420

Milton Argeriou, Ph.D.
Executive Director, Alcohol & Health Research Services, Inc.
134 Main Street, Stoneham, MA 02180

C. Vincent Bakeman, M.Ed., M.P.A., Ph.D.
Kennedy-King College, 6800 So. Wentworth Avenue, Chicago, IL

Katherine G. Barkley, M.S., N.C.C.
Counselor, Creative Interventions Alcohol Awareness Program
109 Faculty Office Building, State University College,
Brockport, New York 14420

Tom Brian, Ed.D.
Counseling Center, Oklahoma State University, Stillwater, OK

Michael V. Fair, Commission of Correction
Commonwealth of Massachusetts
Department of Corrections, 100 Cambridge Street,
Boston, MA 02202

Anna P. Fisher
Westminster Club Apts., E-13
Highway 17 North, Brunswick, GA 31520

Allen W. Gaskell, M.S., C.A.C.
Program Director, Valle Associates, Inc.
183 North Common Street, Lynn, MA 01905

Linda Holt, B.A.
Commonwealth of Massachusetts
Department of Corrections, Research Division, Boston, MA 02111

Joel Katz, M.S.
State University College, 109 Faculty Office Building,
Brockport, New York 14420

Tess Kerns, M.Ed., C.A.C.
Director of Operations, Valle Associates, Inc.
183 North Common Street, Lynn, MA 01905

Albert L. Kramer
Judge, Quincy District Court, Dennis Ryan Parkway,
Quincy, MA 02169

Dr. Robert L. Marshall
Alliance for Traffic Safety
School of Public Services and Continuing Education
Central Missouri State University, Warrensburg, Missouri

Dennis McCarty, Ph.D.
Director, Alcohol and Health Research Services, Inc.
134 Main Street, Stoneham, MA 02180

Robert J. McGrath, M.A., C.A.C.
The Counseling Service of Addison County, Inc.
89 Main Street, Middlebury, VT 05753

David H. Mulligan, M.Ed., C.A.G.S.
Associate Director, Division of Alcoholism
MA Department of Public Health, 150 Tremont Street,
Boston, MA 02111

Deborah Potter, M.A.
Alcohol and Health Research Services, Inc.
134 Main Street, Stoneham, MA 02180

Harold Rosenberg, Ph.D.
Bradley University, Psychology Department, Peoria, IL 61625

Bonnie Spiller, M.A.
Bradley University, Peoria, IL 61625

Brenda L. Underhill, M.S., C.A.C.
Executive Director, Alcohol Center for Women
1147 South Alvarado Street, Los Angeles, CA 90006

John S. Wodarski, Ph.D.
Director, Research Center
School of Social Work
University of Georgia, Athens, Georgia 30602

Maxine Womble, M.A.
National Black Alcoholism Council
417 South Dearborn Street, Suite 1000, Chicago, IL

Introduction

In this special issue of *Alcoholism Treatment Quarterly*, the reader will find an unusual collection of creative and thought-provoking articles related to research, policy, and treatment approaches to one of America's most serious problems—the drunk driver. The authors represent a wide variety of training and experience, including professionals who come from academic, research, correctional, public health and judicial system backgrounds.

The leadoff article, ''Alcohol and Highway Traffic Safety Efforts in the United States'' by Dr. Robet Marshall, provides a comprehensive review of the problem of alcohol and traffic safety in the United States. Most noteworthy is the statistical data base provided in this article which indicates that there has been significant reduction in highway deaths since the enactment of the Highway Safety Act in 1966. With the awakening of the public conscience concerning the immense problem of drunk driving in America, Dr. Marshall's article reminds us of the fact that the United States still has the best driving record in the world. However, this is not comforting when the needless loss of life, injury, and personal and social tragedy caused by drunk drivers continues. Thus, Dr. Marshall provides essential recommendations for improving highway safety in America.

Throughout this special issue, the reader will be presented with an extraordinary array of creative approaches to treating the drunk driver (referred to in this issue as DWI, OUI, DUI or DUIL offender). This is exemplified by Judge Kramer's article ''Alcoholism and the Courts: The Need for New Sentencing and Treatment Strategies,'' whereby a bold and pioneering effort has been undertaken to treat the OUI first offender. This program challenges the assumption that the majority of OUI first offenders are social drinkers and, therefore, would benefit most from educational approaches that increase awareness and information. On the contrary, the experience of the Quincy Court program is that the majority of first offenders were found to have serious problems with alcohol and, therefore, the appropriate response is mandatory treatment, in addition to education. This program also challenges the longstanding assumption of treatment professionals that people must want to get better, or must be motivated, to benefit from treatment. This article compels treatment professionals to examine the value of such variables as coercion, leverage, externally applied social pressure, and accountability in effecting treatment outcome.

David Mulligan and Dennis McCarty address policy analysis issues in their article "Enhanced Services for Court Referred DUIL Offenders." The authors examine the role of court coercion and individual choice in entering treatment, the assessment of offenders and the scope of treatment recommendations made to the courts, and the role of treatment in individual change. Lack of clarity and communication between the courts and treatment providers under- mines the potential impact of court-mandated services and needs to be addressed collaboratively. The authors pinpoint the essence of meaningful behavior change, i.e. clients' internalization of the need for, and commitment to, change, and artfully analyze the DUIL assessment, education and treatment system in terms of its viability in accomplishing this effect. The authors stress that accountability on the parts of clients, the court system and treatment providers is a necessary ingredient for effective DUIL services.

In "Cognitive-Behavioral Group Therapy for Multiple DUI Offenders" presented by Dr. Harold Rosenberg and Dr. Tom Brian, group therapy approaches for multiple DUI offenders are dis- cussed. A comparison of structured treatment approaches and an unstructured therapy group is made and evaluated, and implications are discussed.

Dr. Appleton and his colleagues present a model program for treating multiple offenders on an out-patient basis based upon a social learning theory. The way this program combines gestalt techniques, cognitive restructuring, and behavioral approaches is particularly creative, especially when one considers that the program design lends itself to behaviorally observable evaluation strategies.

Creative approaches to treatment from a statewide perspective is presented by the Massachusetts Commissioner of Correction, Michael V. Fair. In response to the public outcry for more effective strategies for dealing with the drunk driver, the Commonwealth of Massachusetts passed legislation in 1982 increasing the penalties for oeprating under the influence of alcohol. Commissioner Fair's article, "Operating Under The Influence: Programs and Treatment For Convicted Offenders in Massachusetts," explains the changes that have occurred in Massachusetts. In addition to increasing fines and penalties, Massachusetts also established creative programs which have presented new challenges to treatment providers. Some of the issues providers need to be aware of in relating to the complexity of a correctional system are provided in this valuable article. Several articles related to DWI programs and special populations are highlighted in this issue. Dr. Bakeman and Maxine Womble's article, "A Comprehensive Culturally Specific Approach to Drunk Driving for Blacks," provides the reader with the history, scope and purpose of Blacks Against Drunk Driving (BADD), established in 1984 by the National Black Alcoholism Council. The need for culturally specific education and training programs for police, court and human service providers is presented in this highly informative article.

Brenda Underhill's article, "Driving Under the Influence of Gender Discrimination," argues that current DUI programs exemplify the difficulties encountered by women problem drinkers in society and in traditional alcoholism treatment programs. The author argues that the gender-based double standard practiced by the alcoholism service delivery system is even more evident in the DUI delivery system. Ms. Underhill's article provides insight into the basis for this double standard, exposes some of the attitudinal barriers among service providers that enable the double standard to be perpetuated, and offers some helpful suggestions for designing programs for women. The author also notes the need for more research data on women DUI offenders.

This need is, in part, addressed in the article "Characteristics of Men and Women Arrested for Driving Under the Influence of Liquor" by Dr. Argeriou et al. This important research article provides interesting and meaningful statistics based upon a state-wide data base that includes first, second, and multiple offender populations. The data clearly indicates that there is a substantial difference between first and repeat offenders on a variety of measures, regardless of sex. However, the authors affirm the need for specialized treatment strategies to address the specific needs of women, particularly since the proportion of women OUI arrests has increased rapidly in recent years.

An article that also examines alternative service delivery approaches is presented by Robert J. McGrath. In "An Education Program for Collaterals of DWI Offenders," Mr. McGrath applies a concept we have come to realize as essential in all phases of treatment—the involvement of the family and significant others with the DWI population. This article presents a rationale for involving family and friends of DWI offenders in the rehabilitation process and outlines an appropriate educational program for these collaterals.

The alarming problem of drinking and driving among teenagers is addressed in the article "The Alteration of Adolescent DUI: A Macro Level Approach," by John Wodarski and Anna Fisher. The authors describe the problem from a statistical and psycho-social point of view, addressing the multiple factors that impact the teenage population. Demonstrating a solid grasp of the dynamics involved in the problem of teenage drinking and driving, the authors capably propose changes in the manner families, schools, peers, committees, businesses and the media approach the problem.

Harold Rosenberg and Bonnie Spiller address some of the ethical, legal, financial and quality-of-service concerns the field must attend to with the proliferation of DUI programs. Their article, "DUI Offenders and Mental Health Service Providers: A Shotgun Marriage?," presents these concerns in an articulate and thought provoking manner. It is clear that providers need not only to begin asking themselves some of these different questions, but must provide reasonable answers and solutions to the problems related to service.

The final article, authored by myself, Tess Kerns, and Allen Gaskell, completes the theme of creative strategies and approaches to treatment by describing a new and bold approach in treating the most difficult of OUI offenders—the incarcerated multiple offender. In April of 1985, the Commonwealth of Massachusetts Department of Corrections established a specialized minimum security facility for the exclusive purpose of treating the multiple offender currently sentenced to a county correctional facility. The program design and treatment philosophy developed by Valle Associates, Inc. is described in this final article of *Alcoholism Treatment Quarterly*.

It is my hope that the reader will be enlightened and encouraged as he/she reads this special issue of *Alcoholism Treatment Quarterly*. While the topic covered in this issue represents one of America's most urgent social, political, and health problem areas, it is gratifying to know that many of the country's most dedicated professionals are committed to addressing the problem of treating the drunk driver in a creative, compassionate, and accountable manner.

Stephen K. Valle, Sc.D., C.A.C., F.A.C.A.T.A.
Guest Editor

Alcohol and Highway Traffic Safety Efforts in the United States

Dr. Robert L. Marshall

ABSTRACT. Since 1923 when motor vehicle accident statistics were first recorded by the National Safety Council, there has been a steady reduction in the motor vehicle death rate. Since 1966 when the Highway Safety Act was enacted, the reduction in the death rate has greatly increased, or nearly doubled, compared to the 16 years prior to the passage of the Highway Safety Act. Members of the Alliance for Traffic Safety believe that this increased reduction in the motor vehicle death rate since 1966 was due, at least in substantial part, to the development of a comprehensive balanced highway traffic safety program or a systems approach. This article reviews the role of the Alliance for Traffic Safety, the satistical data base related to highway traffic safety and offers recommendations for improving efforts in highway safety from a systems approach.

EARLY DATA BASE

The Highway Safety Act was enacted by the Congress of the United States in 1966. Until then, traffic safety efforts in the United States were not coordinated at the local, state, or national levels. With the passage of the 1966 Highway Safety Act, a comprehensive, coordinated highway traffic safety program evolved. This program, consisting of 18 different standards, is often referred to as the systems approach to highway traffic safety.[1]

Although motor vehicle deaths were occurring in the United States as early as 1899,[2] official motor vehicle accident statistics were not maintained at the national level until 1923. The National Safety Council, located in Chicago, Illinois, first included motor

---

Dr. Robert L. Marshall is Past Chairman, Alliance for Traffic Safety, and Dean, School of Public Services and Continuing Education, Central Missouri State University, Warrensburg, Missouri. This article, with minor modifications, was first presented as a paper at the 14th International Institute on the Prevention and Treatment of Drug Dependence, May 27–June 2, 1984, Ledra Mariott Hotel, Athens, Greece.

vehicle accident summaries in an annual publication entitled *Accident Facts*. In its initial 1921 edition, only public accidents were included. But today, work, motor vehicle, public, home, farm, and school accidents are reported.[3]

Although other organizations and federal agencies maintain and publish accident data, the National Safety Council's publication, *Accident Facts*, is not only the oldest such document in the United States but also provides nearly 60 years of motor vehicle accident statistics in the same format.

Even before the initiation of a national highway traffic safety program, the nation's motor vehicle death rate (deaths per 100,000,000 vehicle miles) was going down. A review of this death rate since 1923 shows a steady improvement in highway traffic safety efforts. See Table I.

For each ten-year period there has been a significant decline in the motor vehicle death rate. See Table II.

Using deaths per 100,000,000 vehicle miles as the base, it should be noted that the death rate—from 1923 to 1963—declined steadily. An even more significant decline in the death rate, per 100,000,000 vehicle miles, was reported after 1966, the year of the Highway Safety Act. It was at this time that a national highway traffic safety program evolved which established 18 highway safety standards. These standards form the basis for a systems approach to highway safety throughout the United States. I will name these 18 standards later in my presentation.

The systems approach may be defined as the application of multi-faceted solutions to complex problems. The systems approach yields best results when (1) needs are identified through reliable data collection and analysis, (2) research provides new knowledge, and (3) the impact of the various solutions are measured and appropriate adjustments to the system are made.

I believe this comprehensive highway traffic safety program as it is being applied in the United States is working—not perfectly by any means, but statistics show continuous, overall improvement during the past 16 years. I am referring to the period 1967–1982.

It is impossible at this time to know with precision the value of this comprehensive highway traffic safety program to the nation. But in order to estimate the effective results of the comprehensive program, or the 18 highway safety standards, I wish to construct a model by making some assumptions. Let us assume that a base year can be used to indicate change in subsequent years. (1) Should that

Table I

Motor Vehicle Deaths, Injuries, Costs in Dollars and Data Attendant to Specific Calculations for Each 10-Year Period from 1923 to 1982

Year	Deaths	Disabling Injuries	Costs	Motor Vehicle Mileage	Death Rate per 100,000,000 Vehicle Miles	Registered Vehicles in the USA	Licensed Drivers in the USA
1923**	21,800	768,232	No estimate	120 Billion	18.20	19,700,000	29,000,000
1933**	36,313	1,279,670	$ 1,580,000,000	234 Billion	15.61	26,900,000	39,400,000
1943	23,400	800,000	$ 1,250,000,000	292 Billion*	11.1	32,200,000	47,800,000
1953	38,300	1,350,000	$ 4,300,000,000	540 Billion	7.10	55,600,000	71,000,000
1963	43,600	1,600,000	$ 7,700,000,000	800 Billion	5.50	82,800,000	95,600,000
1973	55,800	2,000,000	$20,200,000,000	1,306 Billion	4.27	128,700,000	122,400,000
1982	46,000	1,700,000	$41,600,000,000	1,571 Billion	2.93	166,500,000	149,100,000

Source: Accident Facts, National Safety Council, Chicago, Illinois.

*Estimate (wartime)

**Combined estimates

Table II

Motor Vehicle Death Rate for Each 10-Year Period 1923-83
and the Percentage of Reduction in the Death Rate

Year	Death Rate (deaths per 100,000,000 vehicle miles)	Percentage Change from Previous 10-Year Rate
1923	18.20	NA
1933	15.61	-14.23 percent
1943	11.1	-28.89 percent
1953	7.10	-36.04 percent
1963	5.50	-22.54 percent
1973	4.27	-22.36 percent
1983	2.60	-39.11 percent

Source: Accident Facts, National Safety Council, Chicago, Illinois.

change be larger (more deaths per 100 million vehicle miles), it might be taken to indicate a problem of larger proportion in the system. (2) Should that change be smaller (fewer deaths per 100 million vehicle miles), it might be taken to indicate improvement in the system.

In this model I have chosen 1966 as the base year since that was the year when Congress saw the country had a problem of national proportion and passed the Highway Safety Act. In 1966 the nation's motor vehicle death rate was 5.67 deaths per 100 million vehicle miles.

With the 1966 death rate of 5.67 per 100 million vehicle miles as a base and the assumptions previously stated well in mind, I will arrive at a reasonable estimate of the annual savings of lives, reduction of injuries, and the savings in dollars due to the reduced death rate if my model can be assumed to be valid.

Table III lists motor vehicle deaths, injuries, cost in dollars, and data attendant to specific calculations for the period 1966–1982.

From Table III the information in Table IV is derived. Table IV indicates the death rate if it had remained constant for each of those 16 years at 5.67 deaths per 100,000,000 motor vehicle miles; the actual rate for each of those years, or a reduction of 48.3 percent from 5.67 in 1966 to 2.93 in 1982; the actual percentage change per year compared to the 1966 base year; and the estimated number of lives saved per year, the number of reduced injuries per year, and the dollars saved per year.

The death rate dropped in 1967 to 5.47 per 100,000,000 vehicle miles, a reduction of 3.5 percent. This means that an estimated

Table III

Motor Vehicle Deaths, Injuries, Costs, and Data Attendant to Specific Calculations for the Period 1966-1982

Year	Deaths	Disabling Injuries	Costs (in dollars)	Motor Vehicle Mileage	Death Rate per 100,000,000 Vehicle Miles	Registered Vehicles in the USA	Licensed Drivers in the USA
1966	53,000	1,900,000	$10,000,000,000	935 Billion	5.67	96,100,000	102,000,000
1967	53,100	1,900,000	10,700,000,000	970 Billion	5.47	99,700,000	103,000,000
1968	55,200	2,000,000	11,300,000,000	1,010 Billion	5.47	102,100,000	105,000,000
1969	56,400	2,000,000	12,200,000,000	1,065 Billion	5.30	107,000,000	107,500,000
1970	54,800	2,000,000	13,600,000,000	1,115 Billion	4.91	111,500,000	111,000,000
1971	54,700	2,000,000	15,800,000,000	1,170 Billion	4.68	115,000,000	114,000,000
1972	56,600	2,100,000	19,400,000,000	1,250 Billion	4.53	121,400,000	118,200,000
1973	55,800	2,000,000	20,200,000,000	1,306 Billion	4.27	128,700,000	122,400,000
1974	46,200	1,800,000	19,300,000,000	1,280 Billion	3.61	135,700,000	125,100,000
1975	46,000	1,800,000	21,200,000,000	1,332 Billion	3.45	139,200,000	129,100,000
1976	46,700	1,800,000	24,700,000,000	1,412 Billion	3.31	142,400,000	133,800,000
1977	49,510	1,900,000	30,500,000,000	1,477 Billion	3.35	148,800,000	138,100,000
1978	51,500	2,000,000	34,300,000,000	1,520 Billion	3.39	154,100,000	142,200,000
1979	51,900	2,000,000	35,800,000,000	1,525 Billion	3.40	159,400,000	143,100,000
1980	52,600	2,000,000	39,300,000,000	1,511 Billion	3.48	164,900,000	146,000,000
1981	50,800	1,900,000	40,600,000,000	1,544 Billion	3.29	165,700,000	148,000,000
1982	46,000	1,700,000	41,600,000,000	1,571 Billion	2.93	166,500,000	149,100,000

33,700,000

Source: Accident Facts, National Safety Council, Chicago, Illinois.

Table IV

Estimated Savings in Lives, Injuries and Dollars
for the Period 1966-1982

	Death Rate*			Estimated Savings per Year		
Year	1966 (Base Year)	Actual	Percent Change**	Lives	Injuries	Cost (in dollars)
1967	5.67	5.47	- 3.5	1,859	66,500	374,500,000
1968	5.67	5.47	- 3.5	1,932	70,000	395,500,000
1969	5.67	5.30	- 6.5	3,666	130,000	793,000,000
1970	5.67	4.91	-13.4	7,343	268,000	1,822,400,000
1971	5.67	4.68	-17.5	9,573	350,000	2,765,000,000
1972	5.67	4.53	-20.1	11,377	422,100	3,899,400,000
1973	5.67	4.27	-24.7	13,783	494,000	4,989,400,000
1974	5.67	3.61	-36.3	16,771	653,400	7,005,900,000
1975	5.67	3.45	-39.2	18,032	705,600	8,310,400,000
1976	5.67	3.31	-41.6	19,427	748,800	10,275,200,000
1977	5.67	3.35	-40.9	20,250	777,100	12,474,500,000
1978	5.67	3.39	-40.2	20,703	804,000	13,788,600,000
1979	5.67	3.40	-40.0	20,760	800,000	14,320,000,000
1980	5.67	3.48	-38.6	20,304	772,000	15,169,800,000
1981	5.67	3.29	-42.0	21,336	798,000	17,052,000,000
1982	5.67	2.93	-48.3	22,218	917,700	20,092,800,000
Totals for the Period 1967-1982				229,334	8,777,200	$133,528,400,000

*Source: Accident Facts, National Safety Council, Chicago, Illinois, 1966-1982.

**Rounded to the nearest tenth.

1,859 lives were saved, 66,500 fewer persons were injured, and a savings of $374,500,000 was achieved. By following Table IV down year by year, it is possible to determine the same three estimated savings on an annual basis for the period 1967–1982. By 1982, the annual death rate had dropped to 2.93 deaths per 100,000,000 vehicle miles for a savings of 22,218 lives, 917,700 fewer injuries, and $20,092,800,000. When the savings for each year are added together for the period 1967–1982, the estimated beneficial results of the nation's efforts promoted in large measure by the Highway Safety Act are clearly evident:

—229,334 lives have been saved,

—8,777,200 fewer people have been injured, and

—$133,528,400,000 have been saved due to the reduced number of crashes.

The National Safety Council first started collecting and publishing accident statistics in 1921. Since then the annual death rate has dropped, due to traffic safety efforts and other factors, perhaps socio-cultural in nature, from 18.20 in 1923 to the present 2.93 in 1982. If we review the drop in the death rate for the period 16 years prior to the passage of the Highway Safety Act, the death rate dropped 25 percent from 1951 (7.6) to 1966 (5.67). Table V shows the death rate decline for the period of 1951–1966. Those 16 years preceded the Highway Safety Act. The 16 years following the 1966 Highway Safety Act recorded a death rate drop of 48 percent. This is nearly double the decline in the death rate for the period 16 years prior to the passage of the Act.

At this point I would like to make a personal observation. As one who has been working to reduce accidents of all types for nearly 40 years, I have observed that the closer the motor vehicle death rate approaches zero, the more difficult it becomes to effect further change. During the period 1923–1963, there was a continuous decline in the death rate in the United States. This decline accelerated following the Highway Safety Act of 1966. I attribute this decline largely to the utilization of the systems approach. I feel that continued reductions will hinge upon improvement of technology for data handling, multi-disciplinary research and demonstration projects, and continued application of the 18 highway safety program standards.

Table VI indicates that during the period 1967–1982, both of the other measures which are also used by the National Safety Council—deaths per 10,000 registered motor vehicles and deaths per 100,000 population—declined during this 16-year period. The death rate per 10,000 registered motor vehicles dropped from 5.35 in 1967 to 2.76 in 1982 or a decline of 48 percent. The death rate per 100,000 population dropped from 26.8 in 1967 to 19.9 in 1982 or a decline of 26 percent.

Regardless of which death rate measure is used to assess the effectiveness of highway traffic safety programs in the United States during the past 16 years, all of them show definite reductions in deaths and at rates greater than during pre-Highway Safety Act years. In my opinion, the death rate per 100,000,000 vehicle miles is the best one to use since it is based on actual exposure or miles of vehicle operation.

Table V

Motor Vehicle Death Rate (deaths per 100 million miles
of travel) for the Period 1951-1966*

Year	Rate
1951	7.6
1952	7.3
1953	7.1
1954	6.4
1955	6.4
1956	6.4
1957	5.9
1958	5.6
1959	5.4
1960	5.3
1961	5.2
1962	5.3
1963	5.5
1964	5.7
1965	5.6 (5.57)**
1966	5.67

*Source: Accident Facts, National Safety Council, Chicago, Illinois,
1950-1966.

**Published rate carried to two decimals for the first time.

Table VI

Motor Vehicle Death Rates
for the Period 1967-1982*

Year	Per 10,000 Motor Vehicles	Per 100,000 Population
1967	5.35	26.8
1968	5.32	27.5
1969	5.19	27.7
1970	4.92	26.8
1971	4.68	26.3
1972	4.60	26.9
1973	4.28	26.3
1974	3.44	21.8
1975	3.33	21.3
1976	3.28	21.6
1977	3.33	22.5
1978	3.41	23.6
1979	3.35	23.8
1980	3.30	23.5
1981	3.13	22.5
1982	2.76	19.9

*Source: Accident Facts, National Safety Council, Chicago, Illinois,
1983.

1967–1982

Death Rate	Reduction
per 100,000,000 vehicle miles	48 percent
per 10,000 motor vehicles	48 percent
per 100,000 population	26 percent

Single Issue vs. Systems Approach

The primary reason for utilizing the resource publication *Accident Facts* is to show clearly that the systems approach to highway traffic safety has been working. The concern of the members of the Alliance for Traffic Safety, an organization of which I am a member, is that there appears to be a trend toward a single issue approach (alcohol, safety restraints, etc.) rather than a continuation of the comprehensive systems approach which includes the 18 highway safety standards.

The Alliance believes that if certain issues (alcohol, safety restraints, etc.) are over-emphasized with heavy financial support, the remaining issues (or the remaining standards) will suffer. State highway safety agencies tend to stress the issues emphasized by the national Highway Traffic Safety Administration in order to receive available funds. If the Alliance could see that this was truly not the case and that all 18 highway safety standards were being emphasized by state and federal agencies, then the concern would be alleviated. We know, however, that this is not the case. A number of states are seeking to eliminate several of the standards and related laws: the national 55 mph speed limit, motorcycle helmet law, laws requiring periodic motor vehicle inspection, driver education programs, etc. The concern is that if one or two issues are emphasized, the others will suffer or be dropped altogether. We believe this is clearly indicated in the various states today. The systems approach has worked for the past 16 years as indicated by the reduction of the mileage death rate by 48 percent. Every effort should be made to continue the systems approach which brought this reduction about. At this point I should add that the Alliance does not believe the nation should continue the same approaches in all 18 standard areas without any consideration for new ideas, changes clearly mandated by program evaluation, or approaches indicated as necessary by changing technology in highway safety. Constant evaluation and

adjustment in the application of the various standard countermeasures in all areas is assumed. What is needed is continued attention
to all areas so that the system will evolve and bring about further
reductions in accidents.

18 Highway Safety Program Standards

The systems approach includes the 18 highway safety standards
which have been developed since 1966. The standards are periodic
motor vehicle inspection; motor vehicle registration; motorcycle
safety; driver education; driver licensing; codes and laws; traffic
courts; alcohol in relation to highway safety; identification and
surveillance of accident locations; traffic records; emergency med
ical services; highway design, construction, and maintenance;
traffic engineering services; pedestrian safety; police traffic services; debris hazard control and cleanup; pupil transportation safety;
and accident investigation and reporting.[4]

Although these 18 standards represent a proven, comprehensive
approach to traffic safety, the National Highway Traffic Safety
Administration is presently emphasizing and providing funds for
only a few areas such as alcohol, traffic records, emergency medical
services, and police traffic services.

United States Has Best Traffic Record

Even though we have an immense drinking-and-driving problem,
the United States' traffic safety program could be used as a model
for other nations. In a March 11, 1983 telephone conference with
Dr. Robert F. Borkenstein, professor and director, Center for
Studies of Law in Action at Indiana University, he indicated to me
the following:

> During the past five years (1975–1980), all nations have
> been lowering their death rate.
> Americans have maturation as drivers. We have had cars
> longer than any other country.
> We drive more as a nation and have far fewer accidents (per
> miles driven).
> Most European countries require some form of driver
> education.[5]

The United States has the best driving record in the world, as evidenced by a listing of some of the nations in the International Road Federation's *International Road Statistics* (see Table VII).[6]

Alcohol Traffic Safety Programs

When motor vehicle accident statistics are reviewed, one of the factors involved in purportedly about 50 percent of the motor vehicle accidents is the misuse and abuse of alcohol (spirits, wine, and beer). Effective enforcement of existing alcohol laws is needed

Table VII

Motor Vehicle Death Rates
per 100,000,000 Kilometers of Travel, in Selected Countries

Country	Rate
*Nigeria	33
Chile	17
Brazil	16
Kenya	16
South Africa	14
**Turkey	12
***Portugal	11
Hungary	9
Spain	7.5
Greece	7.5
Belgium	6
Israel	5.5
Austria	5.3
****France	4.6
Germany	4
New Zealand	3.8
Australia	3.8
Netherland	3.5
*****Italy	3.3
Finland	3.0
Denmark	2.7
**Japan	2.7
Great Britain	2.3
Sweden	2.3
United States	2.0

*Death counted if the person dies within 30 days of the accident
**Death counted if the person dies within 24 hours of the accident
***Death counted if the person dies at the time of the accident
****Death counted if the person dies within 6 days of the accident
*****Death counted if the person dies within 7 days of the accident

Source: International Road Federation, Washington, D.C., 1980.

to help reduce the problem of the driver who drinks to excess and then drives.[7]

Once effective alcohol legislation is enacted, a comprehensive and balanced alcohol-traffic safety program needs to be developed at the state and local levels. Comprehensive, balanced highway traffic safety programs are needed. The alcohol abuse aspects are but a part of the total highway traffic safety program.

There are a number of elements to a comprehensive alcohol-traffic safety program:

1. *Total Legal System*—police, prosecutors, judges, probation officers, corrections officials, and health officers. The responsibilities of each group should be clearly enunciated.
2. *Adequate Support Systems*—including integrated programs of accident data collection and analysis by the separate states and local law enforcement agencies.
3. *Treatment*—referral, diagnosis, and therapy for chronic problem drinker/driver recidivists.
4. *Educational Programs*—public and private schools, higher education, public information programs, driver education, development of decision-making skills.
5. *Research and Demonstration Projects*—and follow-up utilization of effective programs.

The Alliance for Traffic Safety agrees with the NHTSA statement presented November 6, 1981, which says,

> The drunk driver is a national problem, yet it can *only* be solved at the state and local levels. State and *local law governs in this area* and state and local courts are the only forum for this case . . . the crux of the drunk driver problem in most states is *not lack of adequate laws* on the drunk driver, but the lack of consistent, convincing enforcement of those laws by state and local officials.[8] (emphasis mine)

Under "federalism," there will be an increasing focus on the states—what they are doing and failing to do. It is imperative for state legislators to recognize the responsibilities for interstate cooperation and coordination.

Recent Major Alcohol Developments

During the past two years, two major developments have occurred that have brought together a number of experts from the United States and other countries:

1. International Symposium on Alcohol and Driving

The International Symposium on Alcohol and Driving was held in Washington, D.C., November 17–18, 1982. The Conference Report indicated:

> The International Symposium on Alcohol and Driving brought together nearly 600 persons with hands-on experience in the battle against drunk driving. They had come from all corners of the world to share with each other their successes and frustrations in the fight they had been waging to free their communities from the devastation of drunk driving.[9]

The symposium was sponsored by the Insurance Information Institute and the American Insurance Association. Following the two-day symposium, the Conference Report was distributed. The report detailed a number of strategies for ending or reducing the drunk driving problem.

2. Presidential Commission on Drunk Driving

President Ronald Reagan appointed this Commission in 1982. The Commission was chaired by the Honorable John Volpe of Massachusetts. The Commission was given one year to prepare and submit to the President a report designed to recommend actions to alleviate the drunk driving problem in the United States. After eight public hearings at various locations throughout the country, the Commission submitted its report which contained a number of recommendations designed to reduce the drinking driver problem.[10]

In addition to these two major developments, most states have enacted new laws or amended existing laws in an attempt to reduce the drinking/driving problem. Much of this legislation has come about due to increased citizen support for stronger laws under the leadership of numerous citizen activist organizations such as MADD (Mothers Against Drunk Drivers), RID (Remove Intoxicated Drivers), SADD (Students Against Drunk Drivers), and others.

In an address during the 1984 annual meeting of the Transportation Research Board, Secretary of Transportation Elizabeth Dole reviewed a number of the recent successful alcohol abuse countermeasures programs. She paid tribute to President Reagan for urging community leaders, businesses, civic groups, and citizen organizations to join in reducing the tragic toll drunk driving usually takes over the holiday period (December 25–January 1) and for supporting the National Drunk and Drugged Driving Awareness Week. "The 1984 New Year's weekend was the safest on our highways in 35 years," she reported.[11]

Emerging or Unresolved Issues

Many organizations and/or agencies are identifying factors that may affect the highway traffic safety effort in the years ahead. As an example, the National Safety Council's Traffic Division has developed a list of 88 items that need study in the future if the motor vehicle accident problem is to be further reduced. Other organizations and agencies also list emerging issues or critical needs. Many of these echo the National Safety Council list.[14]

In addition to the problems of alcohol and other drugs in causing motor vehicle accidents, there are other emerging or unresolved issues.

Several issues are developing or are continuing to develop that may have adverse effects on highway safety in the United States. These issues need study to determine how their effects on highway traffic safety may be lessened. We must be concerned about:

1. Smaller, Lighter, More Vulnerable Cars

An increase in the death rate was predicted as smaller cars increased in number and grew to represent a larger percent of the total number of motor vehicles on the road and as trucks became larger and heavier. This has not happened. How do we explain this? Are drivers using common sense? Are drivers being more cautious? Or are there other reasons?

2. Teenage Drinking

Teenagers were involved in one out of every five fatal accidents in 1980. Almost 60 percent of fatally injured teenage drivers were found to have alcohol in their blood systems prior to their crash, with 43 percent at legally intoxicating levels (i.e., greater than or equal to .10 percent BAC). Although teenagers comprise only eight percent of the driver population and account for only six percent of the vehicle miles travelled in this country, they add up to 17 percent of all *accident* involved drivers and at least 15 percent of all drunk drivers in accidents. The Surgeon General (of the U.S.) has reported that life expectancy has improved in the U.S. over the past 75 years for every age group except one. The exception is the 15–24 year old American whose death rate is higher today than it was 20 years ago. And the leading single cause of death (reportedly) for this age group is *drunk* driving.[12]

The above points were taken from 1980 statistics with respect to teenage drunk driving. Since then the incidence of both teenage drunk driving and abusive drinking have been leveling off or going down.[13,22] There are many unresolved questions regarding what the minimum legal drinking age should be.[21]

If this trend continues, it could be reflected in fewer fatalities.

The teenage driver problem with respect to alcohol is difficult to study since: (a) the teenagers are new and inexperienced drivers, (b) teenagers tend to exhibit youthful risk-taking behavior, and (c) teenagers are inexperienced drinkers.[12]

3. Older Drivers

The increase in population aged 65 and over by 1990 will mean more elderly drivers and greater need for special testing, training, and monitoring of them. The increase in the population also suggests more elderly pedestrians with a potential for more pedestrian injuries.[14]

Older drivers tend to lose their coordination, their vision becomes impaired, and they are living longer.

4. 55-MPH Speed Limit

A growing number of legislator, drivers, and others have expressed interest in repealing the national 55-MPH speed limit. The effectiveness of this national law as a deterrent to traffic crashes needs to be carefully documented through sound research studies.

5. Lack of Use of Safety Restraints

Although safety restraints for adults, youth, and children have demonstrated their effectiveness in reducing death and injury in motor vehicle crashes, only about 14 percent of drivers in the United States are using these devices.[15]

Is national or state legislation the only reasonable answer to significantly increase safety restraint utilization?

6. Education and Training Needs

There will be a continuing need for college/university degree programs which prepare needed traffic safety professionals such as educators, traffic engineers, judges, researchers, prosecutors, chemists, law enforcement personnel, health workers, and others involved in traffic safety activities.

There will also be a continuing need to provide short course, non-credit training for various types of personnel such as: accident investigators, emergency medical technicians, bar owners, bartenders, waitpersons, drivers of all types of motor vehicles, alcohol and other drug analysts, and many other technicians.

One educational concern is the need to provide a continuous supply of well-prepared professionals and technicians when emphasis by state and federal agencies for education and training fluctuates with the availability of federal and state funds.

Cooperation Between Countries

In addition to what I have briefly reviewed about U.S. traffic safety many nations are doing much to alleviate the drinking-driver problem. Much more needs to be done by cooperation between countries. Some of these cooperative efforts might include:

1. Legislation

It is probable that in some of the countries legislation may be needed to allow and foster cooperation on this problem.

2. Policy Development

Policies will need to be developed by consenting countries (groups) to permit cooperation on technology exchange, such as on ways of determining the presence of alcohol and other drugs in the body.

3. Total Systems Approach

I would urge through the formation of a cooperative arrangement that the problems of alcohol and other drugs and road safety be brought into focus using the total systems approach as opposed to special programming that results in decreased emphasis on other road safety needs and problems.

4. Technology and Expertise Exchange

There has been a suggested international networking for the exchange of technology and/or expertise.

5. Development of an International Data Base

It has also been suggested that international cooperation and/or data gathering be undertaken in order to determine the extent of the problem and measurement of trends subsequent to international action. There is a need for the development of a more reliable international data base on the drinking-driving problem, for example, as well as reliable statistics on the total motor vehicle accident problem.

Although certainly not all-inclusive, I believe these five cooperative efforts among nations to reduce the problem (drinking-driver issue) would pay rich dividends through the exchange of new knowledge, development of an international data base for ease of comparison between countries, and sharing of expertise.

Let me add that Professor Borkenstein, whom I quoted earlier, urges caution on another point. "You will note the difference between a socially diversified country such as the USA and countries that have a socially homogenous population with differing customs."[20] This statement holds substantial cautionary implications.

The Alliance for Traffic Safety

The question is often raised as to how support can be maintained for a comprehensive balanced highway traffic safety program. How can state and federal funds continue to be made available to the highway safety agencies to carry out their work with pressure from all sides to divert the funding for other essential programs? One way is through organizations such as the Alliance for Traffic Safety. The Alliance for Traffic Safety is a coalition of some forty national and state organizations to promote the private sector's effective involvement in the development, enactment, and implementation of highway safety programs at the community, state, and federal levels. Nationwide conferences on alcohol-related problems reinforce the point of view of the Alliance and its recommendations for a systems approach to the total highway accident problem, including the problem drinking driver. The Alliance serves in the following capacities:

1. as a forum for the exchange of information and expertise among representatives of participating national and state safety organizations;
2. as an educational mechanism for the collection and dissemination of information and expertise among the private and public sectors related to highway safety;
3. as a source of contact for state and federal safety officials for reaching participating organization safety personnel at the national and state levels; and
4. as a coordinator of the activities of the participants, whenever possible, in pursuit of agreed-upon safety objectives.[16]

In recent years, the role of the Alliance has evolved into one of encouraging effective implementation and evaluation of *all* facets of the highway traffic safety program. As evidenced by Alliance testimony at the National Highway Traffic Safety Administration Docket Hearing in Chicago, February 16, 1982, Alliance members believe that the comprehensive, or systems, approach to the highway safety problem, to date, is the best technology available.

The Alliance believes that traffic safety involves a variety of interacting elements. Each of them, when addressed by a comprehensive program, contributes to efficient operation of our highway transportation system. Of equal importance, each plays a role in the reduction of traffic collisions, injuries, and deaths.[16,17]

Of special note is the fact that a comprehensive approach assures the continuation and strengthening of a core of highway safety professionals to address the problems and issues from a multidisciplinary perspective.

Two landmark conferences sponsored by the federal government in 1977 (Airlie House) and 1979 (Dulles) brought together a broad cross section of public and private sector representatives to assess and evaluate the status quo of the national highway safety program. Any intent or effort to modify or restructure Sections 402 or 403 funding needs and program activities should be preceded by an intensive review of the two conference reports[18,19] by the National Highway Traffic Safety Administration, the Federal Highway Administration, the Secretary of Transportation, and the Congress, as well as other concerned parties. The recommendations from both conferences continue to be valid today.*

Federal traffic safety policy must rest on a foundation of national uniformity in those elements that cross state lines such as rules of the road, driver licensing, vehicle registration and titling, traffic control devices, highway design/construction and maintenance, and traffic records systems. That policy should be consistent with the 18 highway safety program standards, which have been the basis of the balanced, comprehensive national program.

The basic thrust of national policy should *not* be restricted to certain isolated countermeasures to the apparent exclusion of all others. This piecemeal approach is clearly not consistent with the record achieved by the balanced program. The traffic safety system at all levels must be viewed and supported as an integrated whole rather than a patchwork. Moreover, it is abundantly clear that state and local decision-makers are greatly influenced by national priority and emphasis. Omission and slight of any major segment of the systems approach are often perceived as abandonment. We view this possibility with deep concern.

REFERENCES

1. Marshall, Robert L., "The Systems Approach to DWI Reduction," 1983 National Conference of State Liquor Administrators, Kauai, Hawaii, June 21, 1983.

2. Baldwin, David M., "Traffic Accident Trends," HRB Bulletin 74, National Academy of Sciences, Washington, D.C.

3. *Accident Facts.* National Safety Council, Chicago, Illinois. (published annually)

4. National Highway Traffic Safety Administration, U.S. Department of Transportation, *Highway Safety Program Standards*, Washington, D.C., February 1974.

---

*Section 402 (local and state action programs) and Section 403 (research and demonstration programs at the national level) are parts of the Highway Safety Act.

5. Borkenstein, Robert F., Professor Emeritus, Indiana University, Bloomington, Indiana, in a Telephone Conference with Robert L. Marshall, March 11, 1983.

6. International Road Federation, *International Road Statistics*, Washington, D.C., 1980.

7. Franey, William, "Introductory Remarks to Panel on DWI," AAMVA International Conference, Newport, Rhode Island, October 5, 1983.

8. National Highway Traffic Safety Administration, Executive Summary, NHTSA Alcohol Highway Safety Program Plan, September 6, 1981, Washington, D.C.

9. Insurance Information Institute and American Insurance Association, "Conference Report—International Symposium on Alcohol and Driving," Washington, D.C., November 17–18, 1982.

10. Presidential Commission on Drunk Driving, "Report to the President," Washington, D.C., 1983.

11. Dole, Elizabeth Hanford, "Luncheon Presentation," Annual Meeting of the Transportation Research Board, National Academy of Sciences, Washington, D.C., January 18, 1984.

12. "Facts About Teenage Drunk Driving," National Center for Statistics and Analysis, National Institute on Drug Abuse, 1983. (Press release by Stone Hallinan Associates, Inc. New York, New York, 1983.)

13. "Motor Vehicle Fatality Relationship Regressions," Dr. William Kling, Economic Research Director, Distilled Spirits Council of the United States, Washington, D.C.

14. Traffic Division, National Safety Council, Chicago, Illinois, "Implications," March, 1984.

15. Steed, Diane K., Presentation during the February 7, 1984, DISCUS (Distilled Spirits Council of the United States) meeting, National Highway Traffic Safety Administration, Washington, D.C.

16. Developed by Operations Committee, April 26, 1982, and approved by the Alliance for Traffic Safety, August 20, 1982.

17. Marshall, Robert L., "Putting the Brakes on Drunk Driving," Address before the National Conference of State Legislatures, Eighth Annual Meeting, Chicago, Illinois, July 30, 1982.

18. Transportation Research Board, *Future of the National Highway Safety Program*, National Academy of Sciences, Washington, D.C., 1977.

19. Transportation Research Board, *Highway Safety Research, Development and Demonstration: Conference Proceedings*, National Academy of Sciences, Washington, D.C., 1979.

20. Borkenstein, Robert F., Professor Emeritus, Indiana University, Bloomington, Indiana, Letter of March 22, 1983 to Robert L. Marshall.

21. A Thoughtful Critique of *An Evaluation of the Changes in the Legal Drinking Ages in Michigan* (by Alex C. Wagenaar and Richard L. Douglas, dated September 1980), Margaret L. Clay, University of Michigan Medical School, Ann Arbor, Michigan, January 9, 1983.

22. Johnston, L. D., Bachman, J. G., and O'Malley, P. M., "Student Drug Use, Attitudes, and Beliefs," Institute for Social Research, University of Michigan, Annual Surveys 1975–1984. Sponsored by the United States Department of Health and Human Services (National Institute on Drug Abuse).

Sentencing the Drunk Driver:
A Call for Change

Judge Albert L. Kramer

In 1982, drunk driving jumped to the top of the nation's political agenda and sent the legislatures of nearly every state scrambling to enact new and tougher laws.[1] This reaction was not simply a form of hysteria brought on by media sensationalism. To the contrary, we were finally awakening to a stark reality that could no longer be denied—for the truth was too glaring. Over two thousand innocent victims were being wiped out in our nation's highways, *each and every month*;[2] over one-half a million people injured, many seriously crippled, each and every year; and in financial costs, 20 to 30 billion dollars were being expended annually in medical bills and automobile insurance claims, all due to drunk driving.[3]

Our attention naturally turned to the courts to see what was being done to deter this slaughter on the highways—and what we found was just as shocking. Offenders with as many as 5 or 6 prior convictions, some even for homicide, were being released back on to the streets (and highways as well) without having served a *single day* in jail. Some were referred to alcohol treatment, but few, if any, were punished for failing to adhere to court ordered programs.

We began to hear from the victims and their families. Together they formed a movement, often expressing their anger in the very names they chose for their organizations—MADD, BADD, RID, etc.[4] They demanded action and so did an outraged public.

In panic, we pushed all the political buttons—enacted new and tougher laws, increased the penalties, cracked down on law enforcement, even initiated road blocks. At first, it appeared to work. Arrests went up and we began to parade more and more offenders before judges. We were prepared to pay the price by making room in our busy courts. The investment has been heavy. In Massachusetts, for instance, one out of every five defendants who appears in our misdemeanor courts is arraigned for drunk driving and these offenses constitute fifty percent of all the criminal cases that actually go to trial. Drunk driving cases now occupy the vast majority of time spent by judges, district attorneys and probation personnel in our criminal courts.

Indeed, we have undertaken an unprecedented number of initiatives and invested significant resources. However, it is now four years since we began and it is now time to focus not on our efforts, but on our results.

On the plus side, the public's consciousness has been raised and greatly sensitized to the dangers of driving drunk. This is no small accomplishment, because this awareness is vital if we are ultimately to change our culture's cavalier attitude about drinking while driving. But where it really counts—in reducing recidivism rates and the number of alcohol related injuries and fatalities—we have clearly failed. We have made little or no impact in saving lives—and when all is said and done, that is the bottom line. Fatalities in the United States for 1984 and into 1985, did not decrease, they increased—by 3% over that of 1983.[5] In our state of Massachusetts, the experience has been the same: fatalities did not go down. After remaining constant in 1984 they climbed by 12% in 1985[6] and another 10% halfway into 1986. What remains constant is alcohol involvement in over 50% of the deaths.

From a criminal justice point of view, we must face the reality that we in the courts are failing to alter the destructive behavior of the hundreds of thousands of drunk drivers who come before us each year. That is a costly failure when we consider the enormous effort it takes to apprehend and convict even one drunk driver. Worse still we must face the grim prospect that these offenders will continue their flagrant misconduct, driving drunk hundreds upon hundreds of times before we get a chance to catch them again.[7] It is critical that we take a hard look at what we are doing, or more appropriately, what we are not doing, and make the needed changes without delay.

First let's take a look at the central reason for our failure. Simply put, we are administering the wrong sentencing and employing the wrong treatment in our courts. The sentencing practices that we now employ are founded on a host of misconceptions—misconceptions as to who the vast majority of drunk drivers are and what it really takes to change their endangering conduct. In spite of clear evidence to the contrary, we keep holding to the belief that the typical drunk driver we see in court is an overindulging social drinker who merely has to be educated to the harms of excessive drinking while driving. It is based on this myth that we have fashioned our entire treatment

strategy for dealing with ''first offenders''—the group that consti-
tutes over 70% of all those actually apprehended—and that has been
a serious mistake.

The program model we now utilize for first offenders is called the
Alcohol Safety Action Program (ASAP) and it consists of 8 (2 hour)
educational classes on the subject of responsible drinking. Overall,
the model assumes that the ''first offender'' is not an alcoholic, that
he is generally law-abiding, that he can be reasoned with on a
rational basis and more importantly, that he can be taught to
moderate his drinking to acceptable levels. Our whole initiative is
based on these underlying assumptions, but all empirical evidence
suggests that these assumptions are completely fallacious.

First, let us see whether the ''first offender's'' drunk driving
violation is an isolated incident in the life of an otherwise respectable,
law-abiding citizen. A Massachusetts probation study (which is typical) shows that most drunk drivers are just as destructive off the road
as they are on them. Sixty-seven percent of all such offenders (44.8%
of all first offenders) were found to have prior criminal records
involving offenses such as disorderly conduct, larceny, assault and
battery, etc., (mostly alcohol related).[8] In fact drunk driving offenders are heavily involved in crimes across the board. Fifty percent
of all violent crimes, 65% of all homicides, and 50 to 60% of all child
abuse cases are committed by offenders who are alcoholics—and a
fair number of these have a drunk driving conviction on their records.

What these facts clearly suggest is that drunk drivers are not mere
social drinkers who happen to overindulge—they are largely alcoholics, seriously addicted, and represent threats to the public safety.
Their alcoholism is usually noticed first at home as a major cause of
dysfunction to the family, then at work, and later (as it spills over)
by the public at large. We see many of them in their first court
appearances for domestic abuse, drunk driving, disorderly conduct,
etc., but usually *only after* a history of destructive behavior outside
of court. Consequently, if we are to initiate effective approaches to
combat drunk driving, it is vital that we recognize the characteristics
of those whom we bring before the courts and then put an end to some
of the underlying misconceptions upon which we base our current
court policies. The most salient of these misconceptions is that the
''first offender'' population consists of social drinkers who just had
''a little too much to drink''—what can be termed the: ''There but
for the grace of God, go I'' myth. Our sentencing has been based on
this myth, and as a result has seriously retarded our efforts.

One might ask, however, "isn't it true that there are many of us social drinkers who are *not* alcoholics, who end up occasionally driving drunk?" To be sure, a good number of us do overindulge and on occasions drive drunk—but the critical fact is that we don't often get arrested. Research shows that there is an extremely low probability of being arrested while driving drunk on the road. A National Highway Traffic Safety Commission study shows that statistically, a driver would have to commit somewhere between 200 and 2,000 drunk driving violations to be picked up *just once.*[9] The odds are very great that the vast majority of those being *arrested* drive drunk on the road some four to five times a week, for several years before being caught. Arresting a social drinker happens—but *not* very often.

Our experience at the Quincy District Court documents that conclusion. In November of 1982, we engaged three of the leading alcohol treatment agencies in New England to conduct two-day clinical evaluations for all first offenders convicted of drunk driving.[10] The evaluation was very comprehensive. It consisted of personality and chemical dependence tests for alcoholism (M.A.S.T., C.A.G.E., M.M.P.I., Mortimer Filkins, McAndrews, etc.), blood and chemical analyses, interviews with family members, and observations of the offender during participation in group discussions. These assessments from November 1982 to March 15, 1985, showed that out of 1,252 first offenders, 1,031 or *82%* of them were alcoholics or problem drinkers and only 221 or *18%* were social drinkers. These statistics are consistent with the assessments made by the state of Pennsylvania. Their statistical summary showed that out of 40,724 defendants convicted for operating under the influence in Pennsylvania (latest statistics up to December, 1983), a total of 78 percent were problem drinkers, and only 22 percent were social drinkers.

Clearly the conventionally used ASAP program model consisting of only 8 sessions of driver-alcohol education—and basically geared to teach social drinkers how to limit their drinking—is totally inappropriate for such a population, even if they are called "first offenders." This population by-and-large consists of alcoholics for whom any amount of drink is lethal. It is clear, therefore, that we must employ sentencing strategies that compel them *to abstain from drinking altogether.*

In January, 1983, Quincy Court began to do just that. The model for the first offender program was fashioned after an on-going experimental treatment program instituted at Quincy Court for repeat offenders in 1979. With repeat offenders it was clear that we were dealing with alcoholics and so a sentencing and treatment strategy was designed to compel sobriety. We were warned that achieving such a goal would be difficult since most offenders would deny their addiction. We therefore devised a tough sentencing policy to be buttressed by a tight probation supervision. In Quincy Court repeat offenders were (and are today) sentenced to 90 days in the House of Correction, with 14 days to be served and the balance suspended provided they successfully complete two years of probation. As a condition of that probation (after release from jail), the offender is required to enter a 30-week program consisting of 5 evenings a week of monitored alcohol counseling and Alcoholics Anonymous (A.A.) meetings. (When the new Massachusetts drunk driving law was passed a 14-day state-run inpatient program was used in lieu of jail.)

We encouraged the establishment of a private treatment program, called the Eastern Massachusetts Alcohol Program (EMAAP) to assist us in this effort. The offender was required to pay a fee of $400.00 to EMAAP for a weekly alcohol counseling session and for the monitoring of his or her attendance at 4 other weekly A.A. meetings. Missing 2 meetings resulted in the offender being terminated from the program and returned to court.

The approach is a form of coerced, intensive and monitored treatment. If offenders fail to comply, they are immediately surrendered to the court and given a series of weekend sentences. After the first weekend is served, they are assured that if they attend their A.A. meetings, the court will stay the execution of the remaining sentence. However, if they fail again, they will be required to serve the remaining weekends. This approach has been most effective in compelling compliance with treatment obligations.

The sentencing strategy was based on two simple premises: (1) if you could get a problem drinker into a daily program like A.A. for at least six months, there would be a good chance of recovery; and (2) the way to get him or her there was through pressure and coercion.

The reason for the coercion is that alcoholics frequently deny their addiction. Denial is a defense mechanism that permits the alcoholic to continue drinking. Compulsion replaces reason. Therefore, the alcoholic is rarely motivated to seek or stay in treatment, especially if it's lengthy. He or she will do so only under extreme pressure—a spouse threatening divorce, an employer threatening a job loss, or a judge threatening jail—and each prepared to carry it through. Thus, the strategy is to apply external pressure to force offenders to attend enough A.A. meetings so that they will recognize their problem and will want to stay with the program.[11] If the offender fails to comply with the terms of the program (i.e., misses any combination of two A.A. or counseling meetings), he or she is immediately brought before the court and "Tourniquet"[12] (short at first but gradually increasing) sentences are utilized to force compliance; a weekend or two, however, is usually sufficient.

The court reasoned that the threat of jail or a shock sentence (when necessary) would compel a fair number of offenders to comply with the very demanding program of attending 150 A.A. or counseling meetings within seven months with the further requirements of total abstinence. *Jail was to be the motivator; A.A. and counseling the means of recovery.*

Of course, the program does not work for everyone. The original fallout rate was high, we estimated about 20%. But getting 80% of alcoholics through the 30-week program, a large number with sobriety, was a fairly good result. I mention sobriety, for our goal is not to achieve controlled drinking. We require the offender to abstain from drinking. Every reliable study indicates that abstinence is the only treatment goal for alcoholics.[13]

Since our evaluation revealed that 82% of all our first offenders were alcoholics or high risk drinkers, we expanded our repeat offender approach (with modifications) to first offenders in January 1983. All first offenders were required to undergo a 2-day assessment at an inpatient treatment facility during weekends. Because of the expense, we later permitted the assessments to be conducted during 2 successive Saturdays, on an outpatient basis. After assessment, offenders are classified into one of two categories: SOCIAL DRINKER or HIGH RISK DRINKER (alcoholic or problem drinker). As a result of the initial assessments, seventy-four percent were placed in the high risk group. As testing became more sophisticated, that figure has risen to 82%. Only 18% are assessed as social drinkers.

Those assessed as social drinkers are assigned to a conventional ASAP educational program. However, the *high risk drinkers* are required to attend a thirty-week program of one counseling session and three monitored A.A. meetings per week. We encourage these offenders to seek agreement from a family member or significant other to be involved in a specially designed program for families. If that family member agrees to attend an Al-Anon meeting, as well as the one weekly counseling session, the program length is reduced to 20 weeks. The reduction in length is not just an incentive for such involvement, we also recognize that when a family member is involved, there is a much greater chance for success in a shorter period of time.

Since January 1983, the program model has been revised by employing more sophisticated evaluations and treatment approaches, as well as methods for effectively monitoring A.A. attendance without transgressing on A.A.'s tenets of anonymity and independence. A number of the nation's most respected treatment programs, including Valle Associates, which presently conducts the court's program, made significant contributions to both design and implementation.[14] As a result, we now have in place an innovative and effective approach for dealing with the "first offender" drunk driver.

Without reaching for anecdotal stories, let me supply some hard evidence for our optimism. Our dropout rate has fallen below 10% and we appear to be changing the drinking behavior of those assigned to the program. A recent independent evaluation of the program's effectiveness was conducted for the Massachusetts Department of Public Health's Division of Alcoholism.[15] The study compared 163 offenders in the Quincy 30 week "first offender" program with 77 clients participating in a conventional 8 week ASAP model program. It was found that the abstinence rate during the first 10 weeks for offenders in the Quincy program was 47% compared to a 17% abstinence rate for those attending the 8 weeks of ASAP. With respect to those offenders who continued to drink, there was a 59% reduction in consumption of alcohol for those in the Quincy program compared to "no change" in consumption levels (i.e., no reduction) in ASAP. Ninety-five percent of the Quincy offenders attended A.A. compared to only a 15% attendance by ASAP participants. While we await a more comprehensive evaluation, the early signs are very encouraging.

Our experience clearly dictates that a new sentencing approach between the courts and treatment community must be developed. In attempting to do so, it is vital that we understand some of the guiding principles which have emerged to date.

First, we must recognize *as a fact* that in dealing with so called "first offenders," we are not dealing with a group of innocuous well-behaved social drinkers who happen to over-do it on occasion. We are dealing mainly with alcoholics and high risk drinkers who drive drunk often and who get into very serious trouble. While many are from the middle class and maintain employment (with difficulty, if we care or dare to notice), nevertheless they are like all other offenders when it comes to their drinking and their destructive behavior. They must be carefully evaluated and in most cases compelled to enter into intensive and tightly monitored treatment for a significant duration. The ASAP EDUCATION approach should *not* be utilized as the primary model for dealing with first offenders. It is inappropriate and ineffective for at least 80% of them. Existing ASAP programs should be altered from an education model to an extended and intensive treatment model, with sobriety and A.A. participation as its central goal.

Second, we must initially incapacitate the more serious offenders in jails or in inpatient treatment facilities if they fail or refuse to respond to treatment in the community. Both public safety and the hope for rehabilitation demand this. For those who commit multiple offenses, we must maintain the incapacitation even when they are released from confinement. This can be achieved by creating what I term a "community cell," a means of tightly controlling the behavior of alcoholic parolees or probationers in the community until they can prove they can sustain sobriety and no longer threaten the public safety. The "community cell" (or intensive probation) would restrict the offenders' opportunity to drink at night or on weekends by placing them under home confinement, i.e., they are restricted to their houses at night by means of a monitored curfew. This would be maintained until such time as the offender has gotten significantly involved in an A.A. program. If the offender is not working, we have often required the performance of community service at detoxification centers to occupy his or her days, as well. Random chemical testing is also employed as a further condition of probation to insure that the defendant is drug and alcohol free. Since this is a particularly tough program it should generally be imposed in consideration of a reduced or stayed jail sentence.

Third, it is essential that mandatory aftercare treatment and A.A. be made as a condition of probation *in every* drunk driving case after an offender is released from an inpatient treatment facility or jail. Ultimately it is the treatment (a day at a time) and not the confinement that will lead to recovery. It is rare that a jail or prison experience will by itself change an alcoholic's behavior in the long run.

Finally, we should strongly encourage judges and probation officers to develop policies that tightly monitor drunk driver offenders on probation. Offenders should be surrendered back to court the instant there is a detection of non-compliance with court-ordered treatment. In many cases, well meaning alcohol professionals permit themselves to be manipulated by their clients. They articulate rationalizations for their client's failure to comply with treatment requirements and excuse them under the assertion that their clients are victims of a disease. They are doing neither the alcoholic nor the public any favors. Noncompliance has a high correlation with recidivism, so all violations of probation should be reported to the court promptly or else we will be inviting further difficulty for both the offender and the next victim.

These strategies and treatment approaches will not come easy. When it comes to alcoholism and drunk driving, judges and probation officers are sincere, but too many are lenient through misguided compassion or perhaps misunderstanding. We are a drinking society and often it is difficult to distinguish the alcoholic from an overindulging social drinker.

How many times have I heard a lawyer argue in behalf of an offender that "he is not an alcoholic, he holds an important corporate job," or in fact, "he has two jobs"—as if an executive whose nightly ritual of having 5 or 6 drinks at a respectable club makes him any the less an alcoholic or any the less dangerous on the road than the worker who downs 6 beers at the corner tavern. How many times have I heard, "the defendant had too much to drink because he was going through a tough divorce," when the odds are, of course, that "he's going through a tough divorce because he had too much to drink." We are all too ready to accept every story, every excuse, except the truth—that in nearly every such case drunkenness is the problem, not merely the symptom.

We must remember that 11% of the population consumes 50% of *all* the alcohol sold.[16] That means that sixteen million adults consume over ten drinks a day, every day of the week, fifty-two weeks a year. They are a large part of the group that we see in the courts involved in drunk driving cases and in the commission of other crimes. However, the underlying addiction to alcohol does not always surface without some probing.

Reforms will not come easy. They will not come easy because it will require us to reach a new plateau in our awareness—a recognition that when we deal with the majority of crimes, we are indeed dealing with alcoholism. It is a fact difficult to accept, for if we do, it will require of us a willingness and a toughness to force lengthy intensive treatment on a large number of individuals whose very disease compels them to deny their own addiction.

The judges, probation officers and support staffs at the Quincy Court know how hard it is for the criminal justice system to implement such a tough policy. Daily, we have watched crafty lawyers circumvent our court programs by demanding a trial by jury.[17] Then, after maneuvering to come before what they hope to be a more lenient judge in the jury court, waive their right to a jury trial and plead their clients guilty before the new judge. All this, in order to escape our tough probation treatment conditions.

This kind of "forum shopping" in order to escape tough treatment conditions for their clients is benignly tolerated by too many district attorneys, judges and other probation people mainly because there is still a great deal of education needed to define for us what alcoholism really is and what it takes to help an alcoholic achieve sobriety. We are all conditioned to be what alcohol treatment clinicians call "enablers," willing to turn the other way and be manipulated by the alcoholic out of an inability to recognize the problem or an unwillingness to confront it. We thereby permit the alcoholic to continue to inflict injuries, pain and sometimes even death on innocent victims, as well as on him or herself.

No, reforms may not come easy, but they will surely come, for the public has been awakened to the destruction and human tragedy that have visited so many victims and their families. It is clear that the public will no longer accept old clichés as excuses for action. They are concerned and will demand a legitimate search for effective and innovative approaches. It is in that spirit that the judges and probation department of Quincy Court have undertaken to bring about reforms in this most vital area.[18]

REFERENCE NOTES

1. State Legislatures considered more than 2,400 alcohol related and traffic safety bills in three legislative sessions from 1983 to 1985 and as a result enacted 387 new laws, a tripling of legislative activity in this area when compared to preceding years. National Commission Against Drunk Driving. *A Progress Report on the Implementation of Recommendations by the Presidential Commission on Drunk Driving*, Washington, DC, December 1985 (see p. 10).

2. Ibid, p. 2: table 1.

3. Presidential Commission on Drunk Driving (1983). *Final Report*, Washington, DC, U.S. Government Printing Office.

4. MADD (Mothers Against Drunk Driving); RID (Remove Intoxicated Drivers); BADD (Business Against Drunk Driving).

5. National Commission Against Drunk Driving, op. cit., p. 4.

6. The Commonwealth of Massachusetts, Senate Committee on Post Audit and Oversight (1985), *A Report: Progress and Problems with the States Drunk Driving Law*, Boston, MA, p. 5. 12.3% is an updated annual figure.

7. Research suggests that a driver in the U.S. would have to commit some 200 to 2,000 DWI [driving while under the influence] violations to be caught . . . " Jones, R. and K. Joscelyn (1978) *Alcohol and Highway Safety: A Review of the State of the Knowledge*," Technical Report DOTHS 803714, Washington, DC, National Highway Traffic Safety Administration.

8. 1985 Massachusetts Probation Statistics.

9. Jones, R. and K. Joscelyn, op. cit.

10. The agencies were Spofford Hall and Beech Hill of New Hampshire and Edge Hill of Rhode Island. Bay Colony of Massachusetts conducted the assessment for Spofford Hall.

11. For studies on the effect of coerced treatment, see Klein, Andrew R., "Alcohol, The Lubricant of Crime," *The Judges' Journal*, Vol. 22, No. 4, Fall 1983.

12. "Tourniquet Sentencing" was first introduced by the author as a sentencing technique to compel compliance with court ordered restitution and community work service under the Quincy District Court's Earn-It Program.

13. The experiments conducted by Doctors Mark and Linda Sobel aimed at changing alcoholics to social drinkers through controlled drinking was completely discredited by a U.C.L.A., Department of Psychology study showing "that all of the patients who had the treatment had failed in their efforts to control their drinking and had gone on to alcoholic drinking with severe consequences." (4 of the 20 participants died, three from alcohol related ailments and the fourth committed suicide), *American Medical News*, August 12, 1983, "Alcoholics Fail on Social Drinking Study," p. 11.

14. Training programs for court personnel were also conducted by Gerald Shulman, former director of Spofford Hall and now Vice-President for Clinical Programs for Addiction Recovery Corporation.

15. Argeriou, M., McCarty, D., Potter, D., *A Survey of Clients Enrolled in the 30 Week Quincy Model Driver Alcohol Education Treatment Program*. A report prepared for the Commonwealth of Massachusetts, Department of Public Health, Division of Alcoholism, 1986.

16. *Fifth Special Report to the U.S. Congress on Alcohol and Health from the Secretary of Health, Education, and Welfare*, December, 1983, U.S. Department of Health and Human Services, Public Health Service, Alcohol, Drug Abuse, and Mental Health Administration, National Institute on Alcohol Abuse and Alcoholism, Rockville, Maryland 20857, Editor: John R. DeLuca.

17. Massachusetts conducts its district court jury trials in a separate court from where judges sit on bench trials.

18. The Judges of the Quincy District Court include Albert L. Kramer, Presiding Justice; Lewis L. Whitman and George M. Criss. The Chief Probation Officer is Andrew R. Klein.

Enhanced Services for Court-Referred D.U.I.L. Offenders

David H. Mulligan, M.Ed., C.A.G.S.
Dennis McCarty, Ph.D.

ABSTRACT. Court-referred treatment and education for individuals arraigned for driving under the influence of liquor are increasing. At the same time, however, there is a concern that mandated treatment may be less effective than desired. Consequently, three issues are examined to suggest strategies that may enhance the effectiveness of the services provided to drunken driving offenders: (1) the role of court coercion and individual choice in entering treatment, (2) assessment of offenders and the scope of treatment recommendations made to courts, and (3) the role of treatment in individual change.

The use of alcohol education schools and alcoholism treatment programs as alternatives to imprisonment for drunken driving is widespread. There is, however, a growing sense that the court-mandated rehabilitation programs have been less effective than anticipated. Reviews of federally funded Alcohol Safety Action Programs (Cameron, 1979; Nichols et al., 1981; Swenson et al., 1981; U.S. Department of Transportation, 1979) and state treatment initiatives (Hagen et al., 1978; Klajner, Sobell & Sobell, 1984; Snowden, 1984) suggest that positive change is usually limited to nonproblem drinkers and that less change is observed among individuals with more severe drinking problems. Consequently, recommendations have been made to increase the use of mandatory sentencing (e.g., Presidential Commission, 1983; The Governor's Task Force, 1982). At the same time, however, arrest rates and the numbers of offenders assigned to education and treatment programs

---

David H. Mulligan is the Associate Director, Division of Alcoholism, Massachusetts Department of Public Health, 150 Tremont Street, Boston, MA 02111.

Dennis McCarty is the Director, Alcohol and Health Research Services, Inc., Stoneham, MA 02180.

have increased dramatically. In Massachusetts, for example, the arrest rate for driving under the influence of liquor rose from less than 3 per 1,000 licensed drivers in 1970 to over 10 per 1,000 in 1984 (Senate Committee on Post Audit and Oversight [Senate Committee], 1984). As a result, more than 20,000 individuals were admitted to Massachusetts drunken driver programs during 1984 (Massachusetts Department of Public Health, Division of Alcoholism [DOA], 1985).

In view of both disappointing outcomes from driver alcohol education and treatment programs and continued increasing utilization of the programs, it seems important to review drunken driver rehabilitation programs and their relationship to the courts. Our discussion focuses on three issues: (1) the roles of court coercion and individual choice in treatment participation, (2) the assessment of DUIL offenders and the scope of treatment recommendations to courts and, (3) individual change and the role of treatment. Although the discussion uses Massachusetts' data and practices as examples, the analyses are not intended to criticize specific program or court practices. In fact, the current administration has taken an active role in efforts to reduce drunken driving and rehabilitate and sanction offenders. Moreover, changes in the controlling legislation have continued to stiffen sanctions for drunken driving and have been effective in reducing nighttime fatalities (Senate Committee, 1984) and rearrest for drunk driving (McCarty, Argeriou, & Blacker, 1985). Massachusetts' data are used simply to illustrate issues that are not limited to a state or region and to stimulate discussion on ways to stem disillusionment and to improve the effectiveness of some sanctions with drunken driving offenders. If one fact emerges from two decades of study, it is that the strategies for coping with drunken driving must be refreshed and renewed continually (Ross, 1982).

PERSONAL CHOICE

The underlying assumption of court coercion into education and treatment is that program participation will facilitate positive change in a number of the offenders. Education and treatment for drunken driving offenders are designed to enhance awareness of alcoholism, their personal alcohol abuse, and the dangers of drinking and driving (DOA, 1983). The primary goal is the enhancement of public safety through decreased drunken driving. Success may be indicated by reductions in problematic alcohol use and rearrests for DUIL.

In Massachusetts, individuals brought before the court for drunken driving (if they are first offenders) are given an opportunity to participate in a driver alcohol education (DAE) program. While the controlling legislation states that education and treatment "may" be offered in lieu of or in addition to fines, imprisonment, and license revocation, an assignment to a program is the almost invariable disposition for first and second offenders. The "may" has, in fact, become a "will" and admission to treatment and education is the expected and routine practice. The appearance of either judicial or offender choice has been virtually eliminated and the sense of favor, gift, and opportunity may be lost.

Ideally, the privilege of program participation should be granted only if the offender makes a commitment to comply fully with program requirements. The obligations must be carefully described so that offenders can make an informed consent to participate. The individual needs to know what is expected of him/her in the program, program length, cost, the program's purpose, and the court's expectation. Informed individuals are more likely to fully weigh the costs and benefits of program participation and begin the program if he/she chooses. Although choice may be limited, there is an alternative that the offender has not selected. A study of a residential drug and alcohol treatment program found that offenders who perceived that they had a choice to participate made more progress in treatment (Bastien & Adelman, 1984). Similarly, the perception of choice is likely to enhance offender motivation to participate in drunken driver programs and to comply more completely with program requirements.

Realistically, however, it appears that in many instances program participation privileges are given without a clear statement of expectations and alternatives. Consequently, offenders may be held accountable for implicit contracts that they entered without clearly understanding the corresponding obligations. The extent of the misunderstanding is indicated by reports from one Massachusetts program that as many as one-third of the individuals assigned to education and treatment failed to attend the initial interview. In another program, 55% of the individuals assigned to one class were missing on the day of admission.

Apparently, offenders frequently do not understand their obligations. Courts, however, also have a responsibility (Presidential Commission, 1983). In addition to assigning offenders to education and treatment, courts must surrender offenders who violate program requirements. Even when the offender rejects the treatment/ education option, many courts do not impose more severe sanctions. In other words, offenders may not only be unaware of their obligations, but perceive a lack of enforcement. Thus, in many cases, there is no intrinsic (personal choice) motivation to partici- pate in treatment and no extrinsic (court sanctions) pressures for failing to participate.

In summary, it appears that courts and treatment programs may need to reassess their relationships. Program effectiveness may be improved if offenders perceive program participation as a privileged opportunity that they enter freely and informed. We acknowledge that while the choice between coerced treatment and more punitive sanctions (e.g., fines and imprisonment) is limited, the opportunity for choosing one or the other must be provided. The choice will be more meaningful if programs and courts actually impose punitive sanctions not only for those who choose sanctions rather than rehabilitation, but also those who fail to meet the obligations of participation.

ASSESSMENT AND RECOMMENDATIONS

After offenders are assigned to DAE programs in Massachusetts, the program conducts an assessment to determine the client's level of impairment due to alcohol abuse. Recommendations are made to the court on the amount and type of treatment, if needed, beyond the educational program. Assessment is a critical component because it attempts to identify offenders with more serious problems with alcohol and, therefore, the most likely to continue drinking and driving. Jones and Joscelyn (1978), however, note that none of the characteristics they examined as diagnostic indicators provided perfect prediction. While a group of offenders with a specific characteristic may be at greater or lesser risk for rearrest or accidents, prior identification of the individuals within that group who will or will not recidivate is not feasible. Thus, at best, diagnosis and referral has been and continues to be an uncertain process.

The extent of the uncertainty is illustrated by data on referral rates in Driver Alcohol Education programs in Massachusetts. During the 1984 fiscal year (July 1, 1983 through June 30, 1984), recommendations for more treatment were made for 44% of those who completed a DAE program. This rate is similar to the mean referral rate reported by the ASAP models (DOT, 1979). However, just as rates varied widely among ASAP sites, recommendation rates in the Massachusetts DAE programs ranged from 82% to 10% of the clients, although recommendations in three-quarters of the program (19 of 26) clustered between 35% and 55%. A comparison of programs at the extremes suggested that, while some characteristics increased the likelihood that clients were recommended for more treatment, differences among the programs tended to remain constant. For example, a BAC greater than or equal to .20% increased the recommendation rate to 95% in the program with 80% recommendations but only to 15% when 10% of the participants were given recommendations and to 60% in a program with 50% recommendations. Thus, recommendation rates appeared to be more strongly influenced by the programmatic environment than by client characteristics.

Examination of client characteristics suggested that treatment recommendations were most influenced by the counselor's rating of alcohol impairment, drinks per month, and BAC at time of arrest. Programs recommended more treatment for 83% of the clients who counselors rated as severely impaired due to alcohol, 72% of the clients who averaged three drinks per day, and 64% of the clients with a BAC greater than .20%. In contrast, 25% of those with no apparent alcohol impairment, 30% who averaged less than half a drink every two days, and 33% with BACs less than .15% received recommendations for more treatment. The influence on treatment recommendations, however, was inconsistent. More than one-fifth of the individuals who drank six or more drinks per day were *not* recommended for more treatment. One-third of the clients who reported BACs greater than .20% were not expected to continue treatment. Among clients with severe ratings of alcohol-related impairment, 17% did not receive a recommendation for more treatment. Apparently, none of the client variables affected treatment recommendations uniformly. Unfortunately, the apparent variability of treatment recommendations and the inconsistent relationships with indicators of need may weaken public and court confidence in the assessments and recommendations. On the other hand, counselors can enhance public opinion by making sure recommendations are consistent with objective data.

Assessment barriers. There are several barriers to making consistent and reliable assessments. First, there appears to be a lack of clarity about who is a problem drinker. In the broadest sense, virtually everyone who experiences a DUIL arrest probably drinks more than a light or occasional drinker. Moreover, because arrest is unlikely, the offender may well have driven while intoxicated on numerous occasions before being stopped. At the same time, there is perhaps only a small percentage of clients who meet the classical physiological dependence and psychological "loss of control" definition of alcoholism. Drinking driver offenders, as a result, cannot be categorized neatly into either alcoholic/nonalcoholic or problem drinker/nonproblem drinker groups. Rather, they are widely distributed on a range of impairment due to alcohol abuse. Specification of problems and identification of treatment needs, therefore, are difficult.

A second limitation to reliable assessment may be the purpose of the assessment—identification of clients who are likely to recidivate. We wonder about the wisdom of focusing on the risk of recidivism as the major criteria in selection for more intensive treatment. Rearrest may be as much a factor of chance, level of impulsivity, or criminality as it is level of impairment due to alcohol use. Would it not be better for alcoholism treatment agencies to focus on a reduction of problematic drinking as the primary goal of the intervention? If this were the case, the only selection criterion for interventions would be impairment due to alcohol abuse. Measurement of success would not be determined by a reduction of recidivism but rather by follow-up studies measuring changes in alcohol use. If the clients who drink more frequently and heavily reduce their consumption or stop drinking, clearly there will also be reduction in recidivism.

Treatment recommendations. If offenders fall along a range of impairment due to alcohol use, it may be advisable to move away from treatment/no treatment recommendations to the courts that sanctify the notion that we are able to distinguish two rather clearly defined groups. In fact, the recommendations for treatment can be arbitrary and even when criteria are clearly defined, they may not be followed consistently across or within programs. Perhaps the DAE system would be more reflective of the reality of client drinking if four or five levels of impairment or categories of offenders were established and the length and intensity of education/treatment alternatives were matched to the client. Clients having less serious involvement with alcohol may only need a number of educational sessions, while more serious alcohol abusers will need an intense program that stresses the need for sobriety. The middle range of drinkers may benefit from options that fall between these poles. Individuals whose primary difficulties are not related to alcohol abuse should be referred out of the alcoholism treatment system to agencies that can provide the needed services.

A system based on differential impairment levels explicitly acknowledges the variety of client alcohol use and abuse. While there is an arbitrariness in selecting five clearly defined levels, multiple levels may capture the reality better than two levels. In all instances, some form of behavior change that addresses problematic drinking behaviors will be necessary.

THE ROLE OF TREATMENT IN BEHAVIOR CHANGE

Whether the goal is avoidance of drinking and driving, the adoption of moderate drinking behavior, or abstinence, behavior change is hard to achieve. Many of us have attempted to lose weight, stop smoking, or alter our behavior in some way. If anything, most of us are probably impressed by the effort required to successfully change habitual behavior.

To change behavior, we must accept the fact that there is a problem. This is not an easy task, especially for the client that has been coerced to participate in treatment, but it is a vital part of the treatment process if the client is to achieve a new behavior. If the therapist assesses a drinking problem, but the client cannot accept the assessment, it is impossible to effectively set reasonable goals for treatment that make sense to the client. Fortunately, our experience has been that many clients will acknowledge some level of problematic drinking. "Owning" the problem is necessary to help offenders/clients establish goals that make sense to them. The goals will vary, but once set, a detailed treatment plan or program that is powerful enough to achieve the desired goal is developed and implemented.

Most people change deep-rooted habits, like overeating or abusive drinking, only through adopting a rigorous regimen that disrupts past behavior patterns and challenges the individual to adopt new behavioral strategies or improve desired skills. For example, to compete effectively in the high jump event at a track meet, an athlete cannot practice with the high jump bar at a low height, but must achieve a "training effect" by elevating the bar in practice and straining endurance. Similarly, the purpose of treatment plans is to create a "training effect" for behavior change, in this instance changed drinking behaviors. Court-mandated treatment programs attempt to structure a treatment intervention of sufficient intensity to disrupt old behavior and replace it with new. Through coercion to participate in a plan, we are anticipating that many clients will internalize the message of the treatment plan and adopt the goals of the plan as their own.

When we speak of "owning" and "internalizing" we are talking about motivation, choice, and will. No behavior will be changed without the internal commitment of the client. We can prepare clients, educate clients, and lead those clients to the threshold of change, but the clients must walk across the threshold of change by themselves. We assist them by providing a plan of sufficient intensity to address their problem, but the new behavior will endure only if the inherent worth of the new behavior is meaningful to the client.

CONCLUSION AND SUMMARY

It appears that when an assessment and recommendation are made to the court, the client must make an informed choice about whether to accept either the opportunity for rehabilitation or the alternative sanction that is more clearly punitive. If treatment recommendations are of sufficient intensity to truly address the drinking behavior, it may be that clients will not see the more punitive sanctions as more onerous. An honest choice to accept the punitive sanctions is preferable to adopting programs that lack the intensity and duration necessary to achieve behavior change.

When a client makes the choice to enter an education or treatment program, it is important that it be an informed choice and that all program obligations are explained. Formal contractual agreements may be helpful in detailing client obligations, as well as the consequences of noncompliance. We recommend that noncompliance be dealt with firmly. As a result, many clients may fail to successfully complete the treatment programs and would be returned to court for an imposition of the sanctions. Conversely, those clients that successfully completed treatment would have been exposed to an intensive regimen capable of facilitating their behavior change.

Perhaps the most important issue of all in this discussion of coerced treatment and behavior change is the individuality of each client. Behavior change is personal, individual, and intimate. It is not accomplished on a "mass basis." That is why assessments and recommended plans must be tailored to each person and that the plans "make sense to" and are "owned by" the clients. We must afford clients the dignity of making a clear choice with respect to sanctions and alternative options, and we must hold them accountable for their choice. If we do not hold them accountable for their choices, we do them a disservice. Clients going through these programs need our compassion, understanding, and attention.

The use of treatment and education alternatives in the court is based on the hope that clients can change and grow. It is necessary to continually review our practices in the area of coerced treatment in order that these humanistic interventions be as effective as possible.

REFERENCES

Bastien, R.T. and Adelman, H.S. (1984). Noncompulsory versus legally mandated placement, perceived choice, and response to treatment among adolescents. *Journal of Consulting and Clinical Psychology, 52,* 171–179.

Cameron, T. (1979). The impact of drinking-driving countermeasures: A review and evaluation. *Contemporary Drug Problems, 3,* 495–565.

Hagen, R.E., Williams, R.L., McConnell, E.J., & Fleming, C.W. (1978). *An evaluation of alcohol abuse treatment as an alternative to drivers license suspension or revocation.* Sacramento, CA: California Division of Alcohol Abuse and Alcoholism.

Jones, R.K. & Joscelyn, K.B. *Alcohol and highway safety 1978: A review of the state of knowledge.* Washington, DC: U.S. Department of Transportation.

Klajner, F., Sobell, L.C., & Sobell, M.B. (1984). Prevention of drunk driving. In P.M. Miller and T.D. Nirenberg (eds.). *Prevention of alcohol abuse* (pp. 441–468). New York: Plenum Press.

Massachusetts Department of Public Health, Division of Alcoholism. (1983). *Standards and Guidelines for Division of Alcoholism Driver Alcohol Education Programs.* Boston, MA: Author.

Massachusetts Department of Public Health, Division of Alcoholism. (1985). Unpublished report.

McCarty, D., Argeriou, M., & Blacker, E. (1985). Legislated policies and recidivism for driving under the influence of liquor in Massachusetts. *Journal of Studies on Alcohol, 46,* 97–102.

Nichols, J.L., Weinstein, E.B., Ellingstad, V.S., Struckman-Johnson, D.L., & Reis, R.E.

(1981). The effectiveness of education and treatment programs for drinking drivers: A decade of evaluation. In L. Goldberg (ed.), *Alcohol, drugs and traffic safety, Vol. III* (pp. 1298–1328). Stockholm: Almqvist & Wiksell.

Presidential Commission on Drunk Driving. (1983). *Final report.* Washington, DC: U.S. Government Printing Office.

Ross, H.L. (1982). *Deterring the drinking driver: Legal policy and social control.* Lexington, MA: Lexington Books.

Senate Committee on Post Audit and Oversight. (1984). *Drunk driving in Massachusetts: 1984 status report.* Boston, MA: Massachusetts Senate, Commonwealth of Massachusetts.

Snowden, L.R. (1984). Treatment participation and outcome in a program for problem drinker-drivers. *Evaluation and Program Planning, 7,* 65–71.

Swenson, P.R., Struckman-Johnson, D.L., Ellingstad, V.S., Clay, T.R., & Nichols, J.L. (1981). Results of a longitudinal evaluation of court-mandated DWI treatment programs in Phoenix, Arizona. *Journal of Studies on Alcohol, 42,* 642–652.

The Governor's Task Force on Alcohol Abuse and Highway Safety. (1982). *Alcohol abuse and highway safety in Massachusetts.* Boston, MA: Author.

U.S. Department of Transportation, National Highway Traffic Safety Administration. (1979). *Results of national alcohol safety action projects.* Washington, DC: U.S. Government Printing Office.

Cognitive-Behavioral Group Therapy
for Multiple-DUI Offenders

Harold Rosenberg, Ph.D.
Tom Brian, Ed.D.

ABSTRACT. Marlatt's (1978) Cognitive-Behavioral Model of relapse and Ellis' (1977) Rational-Emotive Therapy (RET) were used as bases to develop group therapy programs for multiple DUI offenders. The common elements and specific contents of the groups are described. A program evaluation battery administered pre and post treatment found no differences among the two specific treatment programs and an unstructured therapy group on both drinking and non-drinking measures except assertiveness. The implications and alternative explanations of these results are discussed. KEY WORDS: Multiple-DUI offenders; Group therapy; Coping skills training; Rational-Emotive therapy.

Outpatient alcohol education and rehabilitation programs have been developed as one of a number of specific deterrents to DUI recidivism. Outcome evaluation studies of basic education programs for first DUI offenders (e.g., Malfetti & Simon, 1974; Scoles & Fine, 1977) and more intensive, behavioral programs for multiple DUI offenders (e.g., Brown, 1980; Connors, Ersner-Hershfield, & Maisto, 1984), and a review of both "school" and "nonschool therapy" programs at geographical locations throughout the United States (Nichols, Weinstein, Ellingstad, & Struckman-Johnson, 1978), indicate that these programs can increase participants' knowledge and adjustment. It should be noted, however, that their

Harold Rosenberg is affiliated with the Psychology Department at Bradley University, Peoria, Illinois.

Tom Brian is affiliated with the Counseling Center at Oklahoma State University, Stillwater, Oklahoma.

Data gathering was completed while the authors were affiliated with Vanderbilt University and the Dede Wallace Center, Nashville, TN. Portions of this paper were presented at the Association for Advancement of Behavior Therapy convention, Philadelphia, November 1984. Requests for reprints may be addressed to Harold Rosenberg, Psychology Department, Bradley University, Peoria, IL 61625.

effect on actual drunk driving behavior and re-arrest rates is more difficult to assess (see Brown, 1980, and Maisto, Sobell, Zelhart, Connors, & Cooper, 1979, for a list of some of the major problems in evaluation using recidivism rates).

If current public and professional attention to the DUI problem continues to grow, the development and implementation of rehabilitation/education programs is likely to increase as a potential deterrent to recidivism. There are a variety of treatment models or hypotheses upon which such programs can be based—including, for example, knowledge enhancement, Alcoholics Anonymous principles, peer interaction, and fear induction. Unfortunately, in the rush to develop new treatment resources, some DUI programs probably will be designed primarily to meet financial or practical requirements without adequate concern for quality-of-service and protection of client rights (Rosenberg & Spiller, 1986).

We believe that there are two psychological models that may be particularly useful as bases for DUI rehabilitation programs: Marlatt's (1978) Cognitive-Behavioral Model of substance abuse relapse and Ellis' (1979) Rational-Emotive Therapy (RET). In Marlatt's (1978) Cognitive-Behavioral Model of relapse, the presence or absence of coping skills in problem or high-risk situations is the initial factor that differentiates between individuals who continue to abstain and those who relapse. Specifically, if the abstinent alcohol abuser has an effective coping response to use in the high-risk situation, then he or she is less likely to drink and relapse. Alternatively, if an appropriate response is not available in the individual's repertoire, if it is inhibited by fear or anxiety, or if the person fails to recognize that a coping response is needed, he or she is more likely to drink in that situation and relapse. Based on this model, Chaney, O'Leary, and Marlatt (1978) investigated the effectiveness of a skill-training program with chronic alcohol abusers. At one year follow-up, the skill-training group was superior to controls on different measures of drinking. This provided support for the study's hypothesis that individuals who rehearsed coping with high-risk situations would be less likely to relapse.

Although RET is a well-developed set of principles that cannot be described with much detail in this paper, Ellis (1979) has summarized it as

> A theory of personality and a method of psychotherapy that holds that when a highly charged emotional consequence (C)

follows a significant activating event (A), A may seem to, but actually does not, cause C. Instead, emotional consequences are largely created by B—the individual's belief system. When an undesirable emotional consequence occurs, such as severe anxiety, this can usually be traced to the person's irrational beliefs, and when these beliefs are effectively disputed (at point D), by challenging them rationally, the disturbed consequences disappear and eventually cease to recur. (p. 196)

A self-help book that applies the RET approach to alcohol problems has been written by Maultsby (1978).

The remainder of this paper describes the development, implementation, content, and comparison of rehabilitation/education groups for multiple-DUI (MDUI) offenders based on an adaptation of Marlatt's (1978) relapse model and RET principles.

METHOD

Subjects

Twenty-two male, court-referred multiple DUI offenders (M = 2.6 DUI arrests, mode = 2, range = 2–5) participated in one of three groups (coping skills, RET, unstructured therapy) to compare their clinical utility and effectiveness. Practical and ethical constraints precluded random assignment of subjects to conditions, and participants were assigned consecutively in order of their intake evaluation.

An analysis of basic demographic and drinking background characteristics of the subjects showed that the groups were comparable. No statistically significant differences were found among the coping skills (CS), RET, and unstructured therapy (UT) groups on the following measures: age (CS M = 27.6, RET M = 30.6, UT M = 31.0); education (CS M = 13.0, RET M = 10.7, UT M = 11.4); race (CS = 7 white, 0 black, RET = 7 white, 1 black, UT = 6 white, 1 black); employment status (CS = 100% employed, RET = 75% employed, UT = 86% employed); annual self-reported income (CS M = $15,500, RET M = 17,880, UT M = 13,430); number of DUI arrests (CS M = 2.7, RET M = 2.5, UT M = 2.6); public drunk arrests (CS, M = .6, RET M = .4, UT M = .3); experience of alcohol blackouts (CS = 28%, RET =

37.5%, UT = 57%); and experience of withdrawal symptoms (all groups = 0%). All of the subjects in the UT group, all but one subject in the CS group, and all but one in the RET group, had attended an alcohol education program prior to participating in the MDUI program. Also although the marital status composition of the CS and UT groups were identical (3 married, 3 single, 1 divorced), the RET group had 6 men who were divorced or widowed, 2 who were single, and none who were married at that time.

Dependent Measures

A battery of questionnaires was administered during the first and final group sessions. The battery included: Gambrill and Richey's (1975) Assertion Inventory (GR-AI), a Knowledge Questionnaire (KQ), the MAST (Selzer, 1971),the Alcohol Assertiveness Inventory (AAI) (Watson, Maisto, Rosenberg, & Dana, in preparation), and a separate inventory of items (scale 1 to 7) to assess self-reported frequency of: (a) use of alternate forms of transportation when intoxicated; (b) use of a breath tester prior to driving; (c) use of relaxation as an alternative to drinking; (d) use of drinking as a way to relax; (e) use of drinking as a way to respond to a problem; (f) fear of receiving another DUI as an influence on drinking and driving; and (g) spending time to think about ways to avoid drinking and driving. The number of standard drinks consumed per occasion of drinking and the amount of time in which they were consumed were recorded from self-monitoring sheets collected at each session.

Basic Program Structure

All three group programs for the MDUI offenders had several features in common. First, all three consisted of 16 90-minute sessions over a total of 6 months: 12 weekly sessions, 2 bi-weekly sessions, and 2 monthly sessions. Although group members had been screened and oriented to the group program during an initial individual evaluation interview, the first session was devoted to re-orientation to the MDUI Program, explanation of the program evaluation questionnaires, and a presentation and discussion of basic program rules via a pre-printed, non-negotiable contract (Table 1). Although there have been relatively few studies of behavioral contracting with alcohol abusers, a recent review has indicated that contracting can be a useful technique to influence both

Table 1.

MDUI Group Program Contract

Group member's responsibilities

I agree to attend all sixteen (16) sessions. If an emergency arises,
and I must miss a session, I agree to call at least three (3) hours before
the start of the session. I also agree to attend a make-up session before
the next group session (fee $15.00 for make-up). I understand that I may
miss only two sessions or I will be referred out of the group.

I agree to be on time for every session. I understand that if I come
more than 10 minutes late, I will not be allowed into the session.

I agree to complete all homework assignments. I understand that I will
only be allowed to miss one homework assignment.

I agree to come to class sober. I understand that individuals who come
to class intoxicated on anything (alcohol, marijuana, etc.) will be asked to
take a breath test and will not be allowed in the session.

I agree to pay the fee of $360.00 total, with payments of at least
$15.00 per week or $60.00 per month.

I agree that violation of any of the above agreements will result in my
being referred out of the MDUI program.

    *Attendance with only 1 absence (make-up session before next session).

    *Come on time for each session.

    *Complete homework with only 1 miss.

    *Come to group sober.

    *Payment of fee on time.

Group leader's responsibilities

Conduct all group sessions.

Write monthly letters to court agency confirming status in program.

Maintain confidentiality about anything discussed in group.

Send letter of completion to court agency for those members who meet responsibilities

drinking behavior and therapeutic ground rules in this population
(Rosenberg, Douthitt, Sobell, & Sobell, 1982).

Group members were instructed to take a copy of the contract
home to read and study before signing at the beginning of Session
2 (one signed copy was filed in the chart and the client was given the
other copy). They were not required to sign the contract, but were
not allowed to participate in the group program unless they signed.

Although no potential group member declined to sign and participate, non-signers would have been referred to another program
without prejudice.

Coping Skills Group

The adapted model. The program content was based on the
precept that coping skills are the initial factor differentiating the
paths of recidivism/relapse versus control/abstinence. As a guide in
program development (and later, as a component of the therapy
program itself), Marlatt's (1978) model was adapted for specific
application to the DUI problem. As Figure 1 indicates, the adapted
model also begins by postulating the occurrence of high-risk
situations, in our case against a background of control over one's
drinking and drinking and driving. In this adaptation, the risk is of
driving under the influence. High-risk DUI situations include both
the intra-personal desire to drive after drinking (e.g., to drive home
from bars, parties, sports events, etc.) and inter-personal pressure to
drive after drinking (e.g., social pressure to prove one's driving
capability).

Again, similarly to Marlatt's original model, the individual
experiencing the high-risk situation may have a coping skill he or
she can apply in the situation (e.g., calling a cab, social assertion,
waiting sufficient time for BAC to drop below legal limit, making
arrangements for a sober companion to drive, staying over at host's
house). It should be noted that there also are coping skills one can
use to avoid being in high-risk situations (e.g., walking to the
location of consumption, limiting one's consumption by various
means [e.g., Vogler & Bartz, 1982] to maintain a low BAC).
Finally, use of coping skills is presumed to result in increased
self-efficacy (Bandura, 1977) and continued legal drinking and
driving.

If the individual does not have or use a coping skill, a process
similar to the one described by Marlatt (1978) is presumed to
unfold. Specifically, there may be a lowering of self-efficacy
combined with a perception that driving is the best or only method
for solving the situation. As a result, the individual drives under the
influence, is probably *not* re-arrested, and this reinforces the DUI
behavior as an effective means of dealing with the high-risk
situation. The result is recidivism.

Specific program content. Following the re-reading and signing

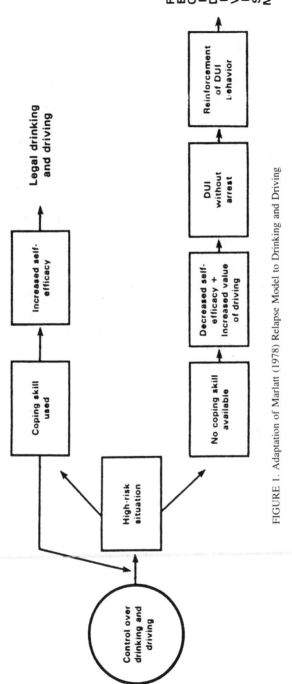

FIGURE 1. Adaptation of Marlatt (1978) Relapse Model to Drinking and Driving

53

of the contract, Session 2 consisted of a presentation and discussion of the state's DUI laws and penalties. (The first of the three pilot groups used to refine the coping skills program included the County District Attorney in charge of DUI prosecution as the guest group leader for this session. Although this procedure seemed to work excellently, it was suspended for future groups because of scheduling problems.) The homework for this session consisted of having group members write what they believed the DUI laws and penalties should be. The rationale for this session and homework assignment was that increased knowledge of the laws that they had violated would provide motivation to avoid high-risk drinking and driving situations and to use coping skills when in such situations.

Sessions 3 and 4 were devoted to didactic presentation of basic facts about alcohol, ingestion and elimination of alcohol from the body, the concept of tolerance, the concept of Blood Alcohol Content (BAC) and a simple formula for calculating one's BAC, physical effects of alcohol on the organs, alcohol's depressant action on the brain, and a continuum-consequences definition of alcohol abuse. During Session 3, a self-monitoring form (copy available from the authors) was introduced as a method of increasing participants' awareness of their drinking and its antecedents and consequences and to provide program evaluation data.

For each separate drinking occasion, the self-monitoring form contained spaces to record: date and location of drinking episode; who the client was drinking with; feelings before, during, and after drinking; time when the drinking began and ended; number of standard drinks consumed; and amount of money spent on alcohol. Completion of the self-monitoring form was a standard homework assignment for all three group programs, although the groups differed in the degree to which and portions of the form that were discussed during group sessions. The homework assignment for Session 4 was to list three personal positive consequences and three personal negative consequences of drinking in the context of the continuum/consequences definition of alcohol abuse described during the session.

Following a review of the homework (as occurred at the initiation of every session), Session 5 focused on presentation and discussion of the modification of Marlatt's relapse model for DUI behavior (Figure 1). Copies of the revised model were given to the clients and exercises were conducted in which each participant generated two personal high-risk DUI situations (which were written on the blackboard by the group leader). The commonality of these situations among group members was discussed, and then each participant selected one of his situations and listed two coping skills that could be used to avoid or handle the situation. The list of coping skills also was written on the blackboard to facilitate discussion of their use in various high-risk situations. The session finished with a preview of the three major coping skills that would be learned in the group (problem-solving, relaxation, assertion). The homework assignment consisted of listing at least three more personal high-risk situations and at least two different coping responses per situation.

Problem-solving skills were the focus of Sessions 6, 7, and 8. Clients were taught the four problem-solving steps (problem recognition, responsibility-taking, and definition; generation of alternatives; evaluation of alternatives; implementation and evaluation of action), and were given homework to practice using the steps with both drinking-related and non-drinking problems. The content of these sessions was generally very similar to the typical problem-solving procedure (e.g., Goldfried & Davison, 1976, pp. 186–207), although several changes were made to simplify the language used to describe the problem-solving steps and to emphasize the importance of responsibility-taking. Sessions 6 and 7 used shaping and homework assignments to help participants acquire the content, and Session 8 and its homework were devoted primarily to practice.

Relaxation as a coping skill was taught in Sessions 9 and 10. Session 9 focused on standard progressive muscle relaxation and Session 10 included practice with this technique plus enhancement of relaxation via imagery. The homework for these two sessions was to practice relaxation for at least 20 minutes per day and record pre and post tension levels.

Sessions 11, 12 and 13 focused on assertion as a coping skill. The content of this module began with a discussion of the concept of assertiveness, the passive-assertive-aggressive continuum, some reasons why and situations in which people fail to act assertively, the consequences of passive, assertive, and aggressive behavior, and the relationship between drinking and assertion. Basic physical and verbal response components of assertion were presented and modeled, and their specific application to drink refusal was practiced. We also experimented with using real beer cans and shot glasses of whiskey as props to provide cues for drinking that would enhance the realism of the role-play and, hopefully, promote generalization to in vivo situations. The third session in this module involved role-plays of non-drinking assertion (e.g., refusing an unreasonable request to borrow money). Homework for these sessions was to practice the assertive behaviors learned in group.

Based on previous research that indicated significant differences between relapsed and non-relapsed alcohol abusers on the perceived positiveness and negativeness of recently experienced life events (Rosenberg, 1983), and the hypothesis that many life events may themselves be high-risk situations, Session 14 was devoted to examining the concept of stressful life events, the relationship of life events and drinking, and the self-assessment of recent life events using Sarason, Johnson, and Siegel's (1978) Life Experiences Survey. No specific homework was assigned, but clients were encouraged to practice the coping skills they had learned previously during the month-long period until Session 15.

Sessions 15 and 16 were used to review and discuss group members' application of the skills acquired in group and to promote post-treatment maintenance by increasing the time between contacts. The final session also was used for discussion of preparing to return to court for one's DUI hearing and the completion of the post-treatment battery of questionnaires. There were no formal homework assignments during these final two sessions.

RET Group

The adapted model. This group's program content was based upon common irrational beliefs as defined by Ellis which were adapted specifically to alcohol abuse and drunk driving. The precept was that change in drinking-related problem behaviors would require change in thoughts and feelings. Therefore, clients were encouraged to think of the group as a workshop in which they would learn and practice new ways of thinking about alcohol and drunk driving.

Program content. Similarly to the CS group, Session 2 of this program also focused on DUI laws, particularly mistaken beliefs and thoughts about DUI laws. This included, for example, discussion of misconceptions and irrational beliefs about blood alcohol level and risk of accident (e.g., the belief that people can drink large amounts of alcohol and still drive safely and be at low risk for accidents). The financial and social costs of alcohol-related offenses were also reviewed. Homework for the second session required clients to write in as much detail as possible their unrealistic thoughts and feelings before, during, and after their DUI arrest.

Session 3 focused on the same basic alcohol information as the coping skills group. The rationale for this instruction was that accurate information helps clients acquire realistic beliefs and attitudes about the use of alcohol and make realistic decisions about driving while intoxicated. The homework for this session was for clients to begin to monitor their drinking using the previously described self-monitoring form. Clients who reported being abstinent were given logs for when they had alcohol-related thoughts (e.g., "A drink would taste good right now"). Again, similarly to the CS group, the emphasis was placed on accuracy of recording one's drinking (e.g., keeping the number of swizzle sticks from mixed drinks or keeping beer can pull tops in their pockets) and the group leader was careful to avoid the expectation that clients would be praised for a particular amount of drinking or for no drinking. This was designed to make the reporting accurate rather than clients trying to acquiesce to what they thought the program leader expected.

Session 4 continued to focus on basic knowledge, including realistic and unrealistic beliefs about alcohol tolerance. For example, the leader discussed the relationship of BAC and the number of drinks one consumes and the mistaken belief that one can always judge one's BAC by how one feels or acts. As in the CS program, clients were presented with the continuum-consequences definition of alcohol abuse. The homework for this session was to list three unrealistic and three realistic thoughts or beliefs that the client had had about alcohol and to continue self-recording of drinking.

As in the CS program, RET group sessions always began with members pairing up and reviewing their homework with one another. Beginning with Session 4, the first part of the homework review was peer-inspection of the self-monitoring form, with a special emphasis in the review being given to feelings before, during, and after each drinking episode. The second part of the homework focused on the self-monitoring of the specific irrational belief that had been covered in the previous session.

An introduction to the ABCs of emotion as defined by Ellis was the topic of Session 5. This was illustrated with group exercises and discussion of how opinions, beliefs, and attitudes contribute to feelings of unhappiness, frustration, depression, worry, etc. and how these feelings contribute to self-defeating behavior (e.g., drunk driving). The group leader disclosed a personal example and group members were encouraged to give examples from their own lives.

For homework, clients were asked to record situations and feelings for which they would identify the ABC components. Also, clients who had difficulty identifying their own feelings were given a glossary of feeling labels.

"Shoulds" and catastrophizing were the topic of Sesson 6. These concepts were presented by contrasting distorted beliefs with more objective, realistic information. Clients were encouraged to identify the difference betweeen a "want" and a "should" (i.e., something they desired vs. something they irrationally believed they "must" have).

The idea of catastrophizing was described as the process of exaggeration of consequences and the development of a negative mind set (e.g., one thinks of all the possible negative things that could happen in a situation until he or she creates a belief that some outcome would be terrible or awful). As clients identified the "shoulds" and catastrophizing leading to negative emotions, they were solicited for what they did when these emotions occurred (including abusive drinking). Group members were encouraged to change the underlying thoughts and beliefs to prevent excessive drinking in response to unrealistic beliefs and negative feelings. Homework required the clients to record situations in which they noticed "shoulds" or catastrophizing during the upcoming week and to consider alternative ways of thinking.

Perfectionistic attitudes were addressed in Session 7. These were illustrated for clients by discussing feelings of inadequacy and incompetence as the result of expectations of perfection, thoughts that one "should" not make mistakes, or the belief that if one made a mistake that meant that he or she was incompetent. Clients were then encouraged to discuss how self-defeating such perfectionistic thinking could be and to explore consequences that they experienced as a result of perfectionistic attitudes. The homework followed the same general format in which clients were to identify perfectionistic attitudes in the ABC format, to think of ways that these attitudes were unrealistic, and to identify more realistic thoughts in such situations. It should be noted that during the review of homework, clients were always encouraged to help each other to come up with better ways to confront their unrealistic thoughts.

The unrealistic need for approval was the focus of Session 8. This session began with a discussion of how society often conditions people to believe that it is absolutely essential to be approved of by every significant person in their life in order to feel worthwhile. The discussion then focused on how unrealistic this is in terms of not being able to have 100 percent approval from everyone or anyone. Clients also discussed how the need for approval had often led to unrealistic approval seeking. This included behaving in self-defeating ways in order to get the approval of other people, playing up to people and then resenting oneself, and looking at how unlikely it is to get approval from everyone when people have contradictory demands. Clients were also encouraged to look at the ways that they dealt with not getting approval (including denial, anger, self-pity, guilt, and depression) and whether they drank in response to these feelings. The group also focused on overcoming the need for approval by affirming one's worth as a human being apart from the value of actions or outcomes and recognizing other people's opinions as just opinions rather than as absolute truths. For homework, each client recorded two situations in which he experienced a need for approval, how he responded, and what ways he might have confronted this.

The topic for Session 9 was irrational beliefs regarding past events. Clients discussed the commonness of the belief that past events are responsible for a person's present behavior. The idea of past beliefs was put into the ABC format (e.g., irrational reactions to present events as though they were identical to past events). Next the group focused on changing these beliefs, especially with regard to the rewards people get from using past events as excuses for avoiding uncomfortable situations (for example, one client expressed that he had been labeled shy all his life and so in a new social situation he would label himself as shy and avoid meeting people). For homework, clients were assigned to use the ABC format to identify situations during the upcoming week in which they found themselves assuming that because things had been a certain way in the past they must continue to believe and act in accordance with the past event.

Guilt, and drinking in response to it, was the focus of session 10. Clients were taught to conceptualize guilt as a form of social punishment used to control behavior. Guilt was portrayed as a self-defeating form of punishment, however, because it generates a great deal of anxiety and denial. Clients also discussed the relationship between guilt and alcohol and the use of drinking as a short-term relief from the feeling of guilt. Discussion then focused on more constructive ways to deal with guilt (e.g., gaining new information, admission and evaluation of a particular mistake rather than defensiveness or blaming). Clients also discussed how the use of alcohol to reduce guilt could compound the problem by resulting in more negative consequences about which to feel guilty. Homework used the ABC sheet to focus on situations in which clients felt guilty and the underlying beliefs that had led to that guilt.

Worry was the topic of Session 11. Clients were encouraged to identify worry as a result of trying to solve problems before they occurred and of thinking how "terrible" it would be if certain things happened. Worry was also conceptualized in terms of a fear of punishment unless one was perfect or did what was expected. The use of alcohol and other drugs by the clients in response to worrying was explored.

As a solution, clients were encouraged to distinguish worry from concern. Concern was defined as a commitment involving the development of options and a realistic contingency plan, whereas worry was defined as a preoccupation with solving problems in advance of their occurrence and frustration about potential consequences. Clients then generated alternatives to worry such as contingency planning, assessment of event likelihoods, and realistic anticipation. For homework, clients identified situations in the upcoming week in which they found themselves worrying, they identified the particular type of worrying, and they generated more realistic ways to approach the worry.

Anger and self-pity were the topics for Session 12. Anger was presented as the emotion that results when expectations are not fulfilled. Clients were encouraged to discuss personal examples of this (e.g., their spouse not having dinner prepared when they came home or thinking a business deal "didn't go the way I wanted" and how "terrible" that was). Clients discussed how alcohol and drugs were ways to temporarily remove the feeling of anger but not remove the source (i.e., unrealistic expectations about a situation or event). Homework for this session involved identifying and confronting personal beliefs and thoughts that led to anger.

Although the topic was not based on a specific irrational belief identified by Ellis, Sessions 13 and 14 dealt with unrealistic beliefs and expectancies about alcohol. Clients were encouraged to explore what they expected from drinking and drinking and driving. A number of expectancies were identified, including relaxation, happiness, being more sociable, getting rid of guilt, and feeling carefree and worry-free. Clients also were introduced to experimental findings on the placebo effect of alcohol (Marlatt, Demming &

Reid, 1973), which showed that what a person expects to experience after drinking may be more important than whether the person actually ingests alcohol. Similarly, clients discussed examples of the power of expectancy effects in their own lives.

To illustrate the power of alcohol expectancies, group volunteers enacted a role-play scene of two friends being drunk at a bar with other members of the group playing background roles (e.g., bartender). After several minutes of role-playing, the clients were stopped and asked to review how they had behaved as though they were drinking alcohol based on their expectancies. The homework for this session required clients to report on what alcohol expectancies they noticed were most common in their own lives and to use the ABC format to report about situations in which they had had specific expectancies about alcohol.

The topic of alcohol expectancies was continued in Session 14 focusing on ways that clients could change their beliefs to achieve specific effects independent of the use of alcohol. Next the clients discussed expectations that could lead to negative consequences (e.g., "If I don't drink at this party, everyone will think I'm not with it" or "If I don't drive home, it means I can't hold my liquor"). A list of these expectancies was generated and group discussion centered around evaluations of how risky each one of these expectancies could be in regard to probability of future alcohol-related problems and abusive drinking. To investigate such expectancies, clients discussed experimenting with not drinking at a party to see if people were still friendly and sociable. The homework for this session involved using the ABC format to focus on negative alcohol expectancies.

During Sessions 15 and 16, all of the topics covered in the group were reviewed and clients were asked to recall and reflect upon what had been most personally useful. This was also an opportunity for addressing problems group members were having with material that had been covered in the previous sessions. The purpose of Session 16 was to consolidate gains made throughout the program and to encourage continued practice of rational thinking. The group continued to examine realistic and unrealistic thoughts and beliefs and the group leader made available extra copies of handouts from previous sessions. Similarly to the CS group, this final session was also used to discuss returning to court and to complete the post-treatment package of questionnaires.

Unstructured Therapy

In addition to the CS and RET groups, a less-structured, client-centered group was conducted to serve as a comparison group in the program evaluation. A group leader was present to facilitate discussion by participants of any topic relating to drinking and drinking and driving. There was no specific program content or structure to the group, except that: (1) the first four sessions also focused on explaining and signing the program contract, discussion of DUI laws, and discussion of basic alcohol information, and (2) the group members completed the weekly self-monitoring forms (but without reviewing them during group).

Group Leaders

There was a different leader for each group. All three were white males, between 28 and 34 years old, who had comparable years of clinical experience, and who were committed to the orientation of the group they led.

RESULTS

First, it was hypothesized that there would be significant differences between the coping skills group and the other two groups on those measures reflecting differences in group content (e.g., assertiveness, use of specific coping responses). Second, it was hypothesized that participation in the CS and RET groups might lead to significant changes in drinking behavior compared to the UT group. These hypotheses were investigated in the context of the degree to which the groups were similar prior to treatment by analyzing the pre-treatment scores for differences among the three groups. There were no significant differences on any of the ANOVAs for the pre-treatment questionnaire and drinking measures except for the Alcohol Assertiveness Inventory Discomfort score and the number of endorsed MAST items.

Significant post-treatment differences among the groups were found for the Gambrill and Richey (1975) AI Discomfort score (F $(2,21)$ = 4.52, $p < .05$; CS $\neq$ UT on Scheffe .05 Range Tests), the GR-AI Response score (F $(2,21)$ = 4.41, $p < .05$; CS $\neq$ UT on Scheffe .05 Range Tests), and the Alcohol Assertiveness Inventory

Discomfort (F (2,21) = 5.12, $p < .05$; CS ≠ RET of Scheffe .05 Range Tests). There were no significant differences among the groups on the other self-report items or on the post-treatment self-reported number of days of drinking per week or the weekly self-monitored number of drinks consumed per hour per drinking occasion (CS $M = .99$ drinks/hour/occasion; RET $M = 1.36$ d/h/o; UT $M = .70$ d/h/o). (Unfortunately, the UT group had quite a lot of missing data on the drinking self-monitoring forms.)

Post-treatment client perceptions of their group and their group leader were obtained by having participants respond to seven-point scale items regarding: overall group effectiveness; overall satisfaction with the group; leader reliability; leader sincerity; and leader competence. The groups did not differ from each other on any of these items, and clients were generally positive in their ratings of the group itself and their leader. In addition, the groups did not differ from each other on the number of sessions attended (all means between 15 and 16). The three groups were different, however, on leader ratings of client participation, using the mean for all clients in each group collapsed across all sessions attended (F (2,19) = 5.03, $p < .05$, CS > UT on Scheffe .05 Range Tests).

DISCUSSION

An adaptation of Marlatt's relapse model (1978) and Ellis' RET were used as bases in the development of therapy groups for multiple-DUI offenders. The results of a program evaluation generally did not find differences among the groups on both drinking and other measures of outcome, except for the significant effect for assertiveness measured by Gambrill and Richey's Assertiveness Inventory. It is interesting that there were no significant differences on the range tests between the CS and RET group means on the two assertiveness scores, even though the former group received instruction regarding assertiveness and drink refusal training but the RET group did not. This suggests that some process or content component of the RET program, which was absent in the UT group, was as effective as specific training to change assertiveness scores.

That the groups did not differ among each other on the drinking measures nor was there any significant decrease in drinking level over the course of the program was the result, in part, of a floor effect (i.e., all three groups began with and maintained low drinking rates throughout the six-month program). The subjects apparently had reduced their drinking subsequent to arrest and prior to therapy, and it is possible that therapy may have helped them maintain this improvement. A no-treatment control group would be needed to investigate this hypothesis but practical and ethical constraints prevented us from including an untreated group in this particular evaluation study.

Although there is a tendency to repudiate investigations that do not achieve statistically significant findings (e.g., Cohen, 1979; Atkinson, Furling, & Wampold, 1982), we believe that the therapy programs described in this paper have clinical utility (and perhaps demonstrable effectiveness that was not fully illustrated in this evaluation study). There are a number of alternative explanations for the general lack of significant differences among the groups that can be considered in evaluating our results and planning replication studies. For example, the nonsignificant results on the self-report items and questionnaires may have been the result of their insensitivity to actual changes in client behavior and attitudes. Furthermore, as in any group design study, differences in an individual's functioning may be washed out in a group average. This gives the appearance of no differences among the groups when in fact some subjects benefit and others do not by participation in a particular program (Hersen & Barlow, 1976). Continued research on the potential effectiveness of Cognitive-Behavioral programs for DUI offenders is warranted using sensitive (as well as reliable and valid) measures and a no-treatment control group.

REFERENCES

Atkinson, D.R., Furlong, M.J., & Wampold, B.E. (1982). Statistical significance, reviewer evaluations, and the scientific process: Is there a (statistically) significant relationship? *Journal of Counseling Psychology, 29*, 189–194.

Bandura, A. (1977). Self-efficacy: Toward a unifying theory of behavioral change. *Psychological Review, 84*, 191–215.

Brown, R.A. (1980). Conventional education and controlled drinking education courses with convicted drunken drivers. *Behavior Therapy, 11*, 632–642.

Chaney, E.F., O'Leary, M.R., & Marlatt, G.A. (1978). Skill training with alcoholics. *Journal of Consulting and Clinical Psychology, 46*, 1092–1104.

Connors, G.J., Ersner-Hershfield, S.M., & Maisto, S.A. (1984). *Behavioral treatment of drunk-driving recidivists: Short-term and long-term effects.* Manuscript submitted for publication.

Cohen, L.H. (1979). Clinical psychologists' judgements of the scientific merit and clinical relevance of psychotherapy outcome research. *Journal of Consulting and Clinical Psychology, 47*, 421–423.

Ellis, A. (1979). Rational-Emotive Therapy. In R.J. Corsini (Ed.). *Current psychotherapies.* Itasca, Illinois: F. E. Peacock, pp. 196–238.

Gambrill, E.D., & Richey, C.A. (1975). An Assertion Inventory for use in assessment and research. *Behavior Therapy, 6*, 550–561.

Goldfried, M.R., & Davison, G.C. (1976). *Clinical behavior therapy.* New York: Holt, Rinehart and Winston.

Hersen, M. & Barlow, D.A. (1976). *Single case experimental designs: Strategies for studying behavior change.* New York: Pergamon.

Maisto, S.A., Sobell, L.C., Zelhart, P.F., Connors, G.J., & Cooper, T. (1979). Driving records of persons convicted of driving under the influence of alcohol. *Journal of Studies on Alcohol, 40*, 70–77.

Malfetti, J.L., & Simon, K.J. (1974). Evaluation of a program to rehabilitate drunken drivers. *Traffic Quarterly, 28*, 49–59.

Marlatt, G.A. (1978). Craving for alcohol, loss of control, and relapse: A cognitive-behavioral analysis. In P. E. Nathan, G. A. Marlatt, & T. Loberg (Eds.). *Alcoholism: New directions in behavioral research and treatment.* New York: Plenum.

Marlatt, G.A., Demming, G., & Reid, J.B. (1973). Loss of control drinking in alcoholics: An experimental analogue. *Journal of Abnormal Psychology, 81*, 233–241.

Maultsby, M.C. (1978). *A million dollars for your hangover.* Lexington, KY: Rational Self-Help Books.

Nichols, J.L., Weinstein, E.G., Ellingstad, V.S., & Struckman-Johnson, D.L. (1978). The specific deterrent effect of ASAP education and rehabilitation programs. *Journal of Safety Research, 10*, 177–187.

Rosenberg, H. (1983). Relapsed versus non-relapsed alcohol abusers: Coping skills, life events, and social support. *Addictive Behaviors, 8*, 183–186.

Rosenberg, H., Douthitt, T.C., Sobell, M.B., & Sobell, L.C. (1982). *Journal of Drug Issues, 12*, 51–60.

Rosenberg, H., & Spiller, B. (1986). *DUI offenders and mental health service providers: A shotgun marriage?* Pp. 153–158.

Sarason, I.G., Johnson, J. H., & Siegel, J.M. (1978). Assessing the impact of life changes: Development of the life experiences survey. *Journal of Consulting and Clinical Psychology, 46*, 932–946.

Scoles, P., & Fine, E.W. (1977). Short-term effects of an educational program for drinking drivers. *Journal of Studies on Alcohol, 38*, 633–637.

Selzer, M.L. (1971). The Michigan Alcoholism Screening Test: The quest for a new diagnostic instrument. *American Journal of Psychiatry, 127*, 1653–1658.

Vogler, R.E., & Bartz, W.R. (1982). *The better way to drink.* New York: Simon and Schuster.

Watson, D., Maisto, S.A., Rosenberg, H., & Dana, R. *Toward the development of an Alcohol Assertiveness Inventory.* Manuscript in preparation, Vanderbilt University.

Creative Interventions for DWI Offenders

George M. Appleton, Ph.D., N.C.C.
Katherine G. Barkley, M.S., N.C.C.
Joel Katz, M.S.

ABSTRACT. The Creative Interventions Alcohol Awareness Program provides innovative and effective treatment of individuals with multiple Driving While Intoxicated arrests. Albert Bandura's social learning theory provides a theoretical basis for the use of behavioral techniques to help group members acquire effective interpersonal skills. Behavioral change in the program is fostered by a gestalt orientation, cognitive restructuring, and experimentation with eleven specifically defined behaviors. The particularly difficult problem of measuring the effect of a program has been incorporated into the learning process, with observable behaviors providing group leaders and participants with a sound basis for evaluation.

The Creative Interventions Training Program, developed by George M. Appleton, Ph.D. and Joel Katz, M.S., has proven dramatically effective in treating individuals who have been charged with repeated Driving-While-Intoxicated (DWI) violations (Appleton and Katz, 1982). Started in 1979, the program currently involves six groups of approximately fifteen members each. More than 500 individuals have completed the program, and their rate of

George M. Appleton is a graduate of Harvard University and the State University of New York at Buffalo (Department of Counseling Psychology). He is an associate professor of counselor education and the director of Creative Interventions Alcohol Awareness Program. Dr. Appleton has extensive postdoctoral work in gestalt psychotherapy, educational psychology, and alcohol and substance abuse counseling. His address is: 109 Faculty Office Building, State University College, Brockport, New York 14420.

Katherine G. Barkley has a master's degree in counseling and is a counselor at Creative Interventions Alcohol Awareness Program. She has done post-graduate work at Rutgers University School of Alcohol Studies.

Joel Katz has a master's degree in counseling, has worked as a counselor with the Pre-trial Diversions program in Rochester, New York, and was an associate director of Creative Interventions Alcohol Awareness Program.

recidivism, as measured by rearrests over a 5 year period, is less than one percent.

This paper will describe the program and discuss the assumptions and the theoretical basis underlying it. The counselor's role will be outlined and leader behaviors designed to foster personal learning in the group process will be examined. Clients will be described, as will the process through which they move in order to complete the program. Particular attention will be given to the evaluation procedure, which combines assessment of individual behaviors with an important learning process for all group participants.

UNDERLYING ASSUMPTIONS

Most of man's needs can be, and are, met through social interaction. Basic to this process is the acquisition of appropriate social skills. In actuality, however, needs often remain unmet. One of Creative Interventions' major assumptions is that problems with alcohol are a result of passive ways of dealing with life's tasks, and that, if a client learns social skills to deal with life assertively, these passive behaviors (including substance misuse) will be discarded.

Individuals who have not acquired the skills to "take care of themselves" encounter frustration and anxiety. In order to reduce the tension and frustration, many people give up the ability even to recognize what they want, and become willing to settle for bearable substitutes. These substitutes allow the individual to meet some needs—the need to be protected from pain, for example. However, they limit contact with others and block assertive behavior. As a result, individuals sometimes lose awareness of their own feeling state, of their own reality.

This is compounded by another process. Self-talk, the unspoken thoughts that a person has about him/herself, limits the individual's willingness to try alternatives to meet needs. A person wishing to make contact with others, but vulnerable and sensitive to rejection, is hesitant to take risks in the interpersonal environment. The person who thinks that s/he is not attractive or lovable encounters anxiety when those attributes are important. The risky situations can be avoided (there are many who choose loneliness over the risky social world), or the individual can focus on the performance of non-threatening, non-self-supporting behaviors with others. Such an internal process may encourage the individual to please others at all costs, even at the cost of self-satisfaction. Lack of conflict, little confrontation and silent dissatisfaction are the result. An assumption basic to this program is that self-talk is extremely significant in the process of creating resistances and defenses, and that it is essential for clients to become aware of their own specific self-talk. Another assumption is that it is not necessary to tackle specific problems (i.e., DWI, alcoholism, etc.) head on. The dulling of awareness through the use of chemicals is simply one way in which the individual may temporarily escape anxiety-arousing awareness. What is important is to teach clients the specific process by which they can become involved in making changes by taking responsibility for their behaviors, including feelings and thoughts.

Clients in the program are not labelled "alcoholics," although they all have a history of repeated offenses which have been associated with alcohol consumption. Indeed, they meet the criteria as set forth in the *Diagnostic and Statistical Manual of Mental Disorders* (American Psychiatric Assoc., 1980) for substance abuse and/or substance dependence. According to a disease model of addiction, insistence upon abstinence is a precursor to recovery or "wellness" for these clients. The assumption that alcoholism is an incurable disease may actually promote the misuse of alcohol and the chronicity of behaviors associated with alcohol consumption, according to Claude Steiner, Ph.D. (1979). In any case, "our current cultural attitude toward alcoholism, one strongly influenced by disease notions, has not led to an improvement in our society's drinking problems" (Peele, 1984). The negative connotations associated with the label "alcoholic" are hardly compatible with the therapeutic goals of a program designed to empower clients actively and assertively to take charge of their lives. There is evidence which suggests that those young men who experience very serious drinking problems are the most highly motivated to change their patterns and the least likely to be severe problem drinkers later on (Fillmore et al., 1984). This seems born out in Creative Interventions groups, to which clients are referred by counselors in a pretrial diversion program (Valerio et al., 1982). These counselors refer those individuals with the most chronic, long-term alcohol problems to other types of programs. Creative Interventions' clients can have a felony charge reduced to a misdemeanor upon successful completion of the program. Pre-trial counselors follow the progress of each client and exert pressure by reminding them of time deadlines, court dates, and specific expectations and limitations of the diversion program. The seriousness of the problems and the structure which focuses on that seriousness appear to be highly motivating to clients.

Perhaps the most basic assumption of Creative Interventions is that there must be a development of group trust before changes can be made by clients. An important element in the development of trust is the demonstration of unconditional positive regard. This helps to change the tenor of self-talk and allows group members to take risks which would previously have been inconceivable.

THEORETICAL BASIS

The social learning theory of Albert Bandura (1977) is an important corner-stone for the Creative Interventions program. One of Bandura's basic assumptions is that social abilities are behaviors which are developed and maintained according to principles of learning. They are, as a result, amenable to change through further learning. The fact that these abilities are here being regarded as behaviors or collections of behaviors allows us to measure degrees of social ability.

There remains the question of which behaviors are particularly important to the socially competent person. Mary Jane Rotheram (1980) has categorized the components which make up social competence into cognitive, behavioral and emotional factors. Cognitive factors include problem solving, the ability to discriminate socially desirable behaviors, and the ability to monitor one's own behavior. Behavioral factors include both verbal (supportive and non-supportive statements to self and others) and nonverbal behaviors. Emotional factors include the monitoring and assessment of positive and negative emotional states.

The Creative Interventions Training Program is designed to increase awareness of these components and of group member's ability to become socially competent. Interpersonal behaviors rewarded in the group experience acquire increased value. Individuals are encouraged to design new behaviors and, through a process of trial and error, select effective responses. This is, in essence, a process of operant conditioning. Because desirable behaviors are rewarded when demonstrated (role-models are reinforced), a system of model reinforcement counseling develops. It is important to note that desirable behaviors are rewarded both extrinsically and intrinsically. Counselors offer support for observed changes in client behavior and, more importantly, the behaviors in themselves produce a desired effect. They have been demonstrated to be useful. Another major influence on the Creative Interventions model is cognitive therapy (Beck, Rush, Shaw & Emery, 1979). Movement in cognitive therapy is dependent on challenging the basic assumptions which clients use to immobilize themselves, to rationalize passivity, to convince themselves of their own incompetence. It is the work of counseling to increase the client's awareness of his/her own self-defeating thought processes, and to provide both opportunity and tools with which to challenge (change) the process. According to Beck et al. (1979, p. 118):

> There is no easy way to "talk the patient out" of his conclusions that he is weak, inept or vacuous. . . . By helping the patient change certain behaviors the therapist may demonstrate to the patient that his negative, over-generalized conclusions were incorrect. Following specific behavior changes the therapist may show the patient that . . . his discouragement and pessimism make it difficult to mobilize his resources and make the necessary effort. The patient thereby comes to recognize that the source of his problem is a cognitive error. He *thinks* (incorrectly) that he is inept, weak and helpless, and those beliefs seriously restrict his motivation and behavior.

Assumptions basic to gestalt therapy provide a third major influence on the Creative Interventions program. According to this theory, the interpersonal life tasks which clients encounter in the outside world may be related to encounters in the group. If difficulties in interpersonal behaviors exist, these "problem" behaviors will show up and can be dealt with in the present. Present awareness is, therefore, emphasized. Because the client's characteristic ways of handling (and causing) stress become apparent in the process, specific problems become irrelevant. What is important is the awareness of the ways in which the client forces him/herself to experience (and react to) stressful situations.

Since whatever happens in an experiential group can, and should, afford the individual the opportunity to learn how s/he reacts in interpersonal situations, the entirety of the group experience is important. It is particularly important that the group member become aware of how s/he reacts in periods of stress. Because such stress as does exist in the group is invaluable in the learning process, it is often useful to introduce difficulties purposely. At that time inappropriate or non-useful behaviors may be manifested.

According to gestalt theory, many behaviors which develop in childhood as creative responses to difficult, unpleasant, threatening, situations become ingrained in the adult's behavioral repertoire as resistances. These once useful behaviors are now often misdirected, serving to disconnect the individual from meaningful portions of the interpersonal environment. The Poslters (1973, p. 71) point out that the result is a "diverted interaction," rather than a contactful interaction with the environment. Perls, Hefferline and Goodman (1951, p. 173) point out that, as adults we have the opportunity to change: "We are bigger, stronger, and we have rights which are denied children. In these drastically changed circumstances it is worth having another try at getting what we need from the environment."

For change to occur it is essential that resistances be recognized and under aware control. Effective behaviors must be found to replace misdirected ones. Feedback to the client as to the effectiveness (or ineffectiveness) of his/her behaviors then becomes the vehicle for implementing change. The strategy behind the group experience is to provide clients with a situation in which they can try out new behaviors and eliminate some of the restrictive beliefs they hold. They can then permit themselves to reach the highly valued state of self-reliance.

PROGRAM DESIGN

Basic to the process of change is the recognition by the individual of his/her responsibility to take care of him/herself and to meet needs through direct action, not through the manipulation of others or at the expense of others. To provide guidelines for group members on acceptable, productive behaviors, each is given a list of eleven "behavioral competencies." Cognitive, behavioral and emotional factors are all involved in specific, observable behaviors which individuals are expected to practice regularly in the group. The competencies serve as a framework within which the client is able to collaborate actively in the cognitive restructuring which is deemed essential to the process of change. The competencies, with some definition, follow.

Giving feedback—making a statement about how a group mem-

ber's present behavior affects you. This involves paying attention to non-verbal behavior in others (tone of voice, silence, posture, gestures, etc.). It is important that feedback be comprised of three parts: the description of a specific behavior, an explanation of the thoughts elicited by the behavior, and the naming of the feelings that result from aforesaid thought process. Feedback thus given does not blame its recipient for any other person's feelings. It *does* provide an opportunity to discover the effect that specific behaviors have on others, and s/he may or may not wish to change behaviors subsequently.

Being responsible—seeing yourself as causing your own feelings and as having a choice in the way you behave. In communicating the thoughts elicited by specific behaviors and naming resultant feelings, the giver of feedback develops an understanding of this competency.

Demonstrating to others that you can understand their feelings, understand the way they see a situation, and hear them accurately. In responding to feedback, an individual has a perfect opportunity to practice this competency. Counselors pay close attention to responses to feedback because clients often deny, excuse, or explain away the behaviors they have received feedback on. These are ways of "wiping out" feedback and rendering it ineffective. When Jim is told that he does not appear to be taking responsibility for his part in the process of getting angry, he replies, "Well, I meant it right. I just didn't say it right. That's because I'm really tired tonight." Jim has effectively told himself that he does not have to listen to the feedback. As a result there is no need for him to change his behavior in the future. He can continue to see the environment as the source of his anger.

Self-disclosing—demonstrating the ability to communicate your thoughts and feelings in the immediate present to others. Clients have little difficulty disclosing pleasant or neutral feelings in the present. "Now I feel comfortable with you," is often heard in group meetings. It seems not too difficult for most clients to disclose unpleasant affect from "out there": anger at the boss, grief, etc. The truly difficult self-disclosure is of strong, unpleasant emotions, such as anger and fear, that come up in the group. Until an individual learns to disclose discomforts as they occur, s/he cannot be truly effective interpersonally, and feelings of anxiety will result from "unfinished business."

Making connections and seeing similarities between your

thoughts, feelings, and behavior in the group, and your thoughts, feelings, and behavior outside the group. It is important that a client come to recognize the *process* by which s/he gets in trouble, realize that it is a process that occurs wherever s/he may be, and learn to change that process.

Congruency—having your words and nonverbal behavior communicating the same thing to others. Incongruent behaviors are a signal of conflicting needs and can be used to help an individual get in touch with, and express, true feelings. In addition, learning to notice incongruency provides group members with another tool to increase effective communication.

Experimenting with new behaviors. Meeting any of the competencies may require experimenting with new behaviors. Other new behaviors might include speaking more loudly, more softly, more or less often.

Finding ways of helping group members who do not meet the competencies. The most helpful behaviors in this case are those required by other competencies, especially giving feedback and/or self-disclosing. Non-supportive feedback is particularly effective in helping others to meet competencies. Ineffective attempts include asking questions or giving advice. Group leaders frequently point out that a question asked passes up an opportunity for giving feedback. For example, "Bob, what's going on with you?" could be more productively stated:

> Bob, you haven't said a word today, and the expression on your face hasn't changed at all. That makes me think that you aren't even paying attention. Since it's my evaluation, I feel kind of angry at you for not getting involved, and I'm starting to worry that I'm not doing a very good job tonight.

Advice giving is, at best, useless. Creative Interventions counselors sometimes point out that, if advice worked, no one would have been required to participate in the program. Anyone who has had more than one DWI arrest has surely received plenty of advice. A more damning drawback is that the giver of advice does not seem to trust that the receiver is capable of figuring out what to do, yet is unwilling to disclose this lack of trust. This underlying condescension is counterproductive to healthy social interaction.

Demonstrating basic assertiveness skills, actively and directly, to make changes in the group. New group members are often unaware of the distinctions between passive, assertive, and aggressive behaviors. Learning that assertive behaviors are most useful in making interpersonal changes is important.

Most difficult to meet of the competencies are *identify the process you go through and the thoughts you have about yourself when you want to drink,* and *demonstrate behaviors in the group which show that you can change that process and those thoughts.* An adequate demonstration of these competencies requires that the group member understand all of the other nine, have demonstrated them regularly, and have integrated self-learning and a new cognitive-behavioral system. One result of this integration of cognitions, behaviors and feelings is that the individual now recognizes his responsibility and power in the meeting of his/her needs. S/he has become aware of self-talk and is now able to change the self-destructive process.

THE PROCESS OF RECOVERY

The process of recovery requires a minimum of twenty weeks. That it usually takes from six to twelve months of practice before new behaviors are thoroughly integrated is pointed out by Gary Emery (1980, p. 260). After ten weeks a client may ask for an evaluation in which other group members give feedback as to how s/he is or is not meeting the competencies. At the twentieth week of attendance, and at five week intervals thereafter, a member may ask others to support a group decision that s/he is ready to leave the group, having regularly demonstrated the required competencies.

Clients move through stages which are roughly similar for all. Not everyone moves at the same pace. Some seem to pass through particular stages relatively quickly, only to remain "stuck" in others for a disproportionately long time. Many move backward in the cycle or demonstrate isolated cases of behavior characteristic of early stages. This is most likely to happen in periods of high stress. Experience indicates that it is necessary, however, to pass through all of the stages, and that they do occur in roughly the same order.

The first stage is one of acclimation. New members are often withdrawn and silent. When they do speak, they are apt to express confusion, dissatisfaction and helplessness. In the second stage they express anger and blaming toward group leaders, group membership, DWI arrests and the legal system. Feedback, if given, is superficial and generally not useful. In the third stage group members, who are becoming aware that self-disclosure is important, begin to deal with feelings. Self-disclosures at this time are often about incidents from the past and/or from outside the group. Many excuses are made for non-performance of competencies. Interactions are often abrupt and clumsy. However, the individual is willing to take risks in spite of confusion and imperfect understanding. In the fourth stage the focus begins to be on the present. Moment-to-moment disclosure becomes possible and progressively easier. Assertive behavior increases and the self-assurance of the member rises. The value of non-supportive feedback as a prerequisite to behavioral change is accepted, and a willingness to give it is demonstrated. Experimentation with new behaviors is now acceptable and, sometimes, regarded as fun. The fifth stage is identified by a display of productive behaviors and by a willingness to listen to non-supportive feedback, and to change behaviors as a result. Individuals at this stage demonstrate awareness of their power to make changes in the group through effective, present-oriented interventions. Interactions are appropriate and constructive, while trust in the group process is apparent. Group members now demonstrate all of the competencies on a regular basis. Self-acceptance and an understanding of responsibility are clearly shown. Some group members continue to drink, some choose to abstain, but none see alcohol as the problem. Its misuse is regarded as a symptom of an underlying, irrational philosophy. Because the individual has become more aware and learned new behaviors to replace his/her self-defeating processes with constructive processes, irresponsible use of alcohol no longer occurs.

THE FINAL EVALUATION

A properly conducted final evaluation is usually a representation of the process which has taken place with the client. It shows, quite clearly, just what stage of recovery has been reached by the individual. The competencies must have been demonstrated regularly for at least five weeks by the person being evaluated, and must continue to be demonstrated throughout the evaluation process, if the client is to obtain a group consensus that s/he is ready to leave the group. In short, the evaluation is a demonstration of the degree to which the individual can meet his/her needs in an interpersonal situation.

If the person being evaluated does not demonstrate the competencies, the evaluation will flounder. Group members who are truly aware of the competencies will give feedback focusing on non-facilitative behaviors, and will not agree to support a group decision that the individual should be permitted to leave the group. Indeed, it is important for group members to withhold support if they, themselves, wish to demonstrate competencies.

The most difficult competencies to meet are *identify the process you go through and the thoughts you have about yourself when you want to drink*, and *demonstrate behaviors in the group which show that you can change that process and those thoughts*. Experience indicates that, unless the group member has been demonstrating all of the other competencies and clearly understands their implications, it is not possible to meet these requirements. In fact, if new and more adaptive behaviors have not been learned, the behaviors (including thought processes) associated with the original drinking problem will emerge in interpersonal situations characterized by stress. Final evaluations are just such situations, and provide opportunities for learning for the entire group membership.

An illustration of this point takes place in Steve's evaluation. Steve begins by talking about how he has met the competencies and how they have changed his life. He is excited and happy and feels very good about himself now that he has learned to take care of himself. However, when he talks about his process, he fails to deal adequately with it. He talks about wanting to be accepted by a group of wealthy, influential friends who drank a great deal. He says that he thought he had to drink to be accepted and to get the courage to interact with them. There are elements in his thinking which are common to many group members. Steve puts the problem "out there," on his friends, and seems to release himself from responsibility. He does *not* deal with thoughts about himself, only with consequent feelings of insecurity and inferiority. *He does not disclose how he generates these feelings with specific thoughts.*

What stands out or becomes "figure" here is Steve's inability to see himself as acceptable unless he becomes part of and adopts uncritically the behaviors of a group. Certain actions of Steve's in the group seem to indicate his confluence. They seem to be directed toward compliance with his fantasies about the group's expectations of him.

As the evaluation proceeds, it becomes apparent that a particular process is occurring in the group. Steve receives a great deal of supportive feedback. As one of the group's strongest and most influential members, his inadequacies seem not to be apparent to newer, less sophisticated, clients. In fact, group members express an emotional investment in Steve's leaving the group. He is someone they look up to, a symbol of what they hope to become. They are nearly wholehearted in their support of him. Steve, in turn, gives much supportive feedback to other group members, *and ignores or overlooks a number of important occurrences* which might have required him to give nonsupportive feedback.

Stress is introduced into the situation after about an hour of mutually expressed support. A counselor points out that several significant behaviors have not been dealt with. (1) Jim's feedback to Steve had included several contradictory statements as to how well Steve was meeting competencies. Steve chose to explain away nonsupportive comments, or to ignore them completely, and focused on the supportive statements. Jim (a new member) often sounded angry and bitter, and made irresponsible statements which seemed to blame others for his predicament. Steve ignored both the affect and the irresponsibility. (2) Another fairly new member, Bob, stated that he did not have a problem with drinking "like the rest of you guys. My problem is that I go out too much." When Sandy confronted Bob on this statement, Steve said, "Let's get back to my evaluation." In this way he failed to help either Bob or Sandy, did not deal with affect in the present, and met no competencies. (3) Several times during the evening, it was apaprent that the group was avoiding issues by engaging in off-task conversation . . . talking about things, focusing on outside incidents, etc. At these times Steve made no attempt to redirect the group.

The counselor's feedback is dismissed by Steve, who says that he does not think any of those behaviors were very important. At this point, the counselor remarks on the similarity between what has been happening in the group and what Steve has described as the process that got him in trouble in the first place. Steve's behaviors seem directed toward keeping the group safe, warm, and loving. Any sign of dissonance is immediately smoothed over or evaded by Steve, instead of being confronted in a straightforward way. Steve fails to self-disclose, in the present. The counselor states that she cannot help but wonder if Steve is trying to make himself and his behaviors acceptable to the group, just as when he drank irresponsibly, and that these thoughts are making her doubtful of Steve's readiness to leave the group. Upon this confrontation, many group members spring to Steve's defense. Steve denies the importance of the counselor's observations and proclaims that he does not care what anyone else thinks, that he knows he has changed and that he is ready to leave the group.

He is then told by a counselor that he will not be able to change his self-defeating processes until he is able to be *specific* about the process he goes through and the thoughts he has about himself. In response, Steve continues to say that he knows he has successfully met all competencies, in spite of views to the contrary. Numerous times he tackles the competencies again, becoming more vague with each attempt. Eventually, the leaders compare the necessity for specificity in self-talk with the need for specificity in feedback. The example is given:

> If you tell someone, "I don't like you. I think you're dumb," you are not doing anything to promote resolution of your problems. If you are more specific and say, "When I made that suggestion, you rejected it immediately. I don't believe you even thought about it. I've noticed that you often respond to my suggestions like that, and I'm starting to think you don't have any respect for me or for my ideas. I am hurt, and I feel pretty angry too," then the person you are talking to knows exactly what behaviors you object to. You have a chance to resolve your difficulties. The same concept applies to self-talk. When talking to yourself, if you say something non-specific, like "I'm too dumb for these people," then you do not have the information you need to interrupt the process.

Steve listens, then continues to make vague statements about his process. He says he "thought he was a 'stupid ass,'" but seems unable to focus on how he reached this conclusion or what being a "stupid ass" means to him. Eventually, a leader gives a precise example of his own self-talk. He says that, driving home from group, he might well say to himself:

> Damn! You really screwed up tonight. The group seems to be slipping, and it's all your fault. You talk too much! Why can't you just keep your mouth shut? No, you have to intellectualize and lead the group off track. You're so impatient! And

egocentric! You didn't give anybody a chance to work things through for themselves. When will you ever learn? What a lousy group leader you are! It's lucky for you that they don't really know what you're supposed to be doing!

The leader discloses that such self-talk makes him so anxious and distressed that he wants nothing more than to shut it out. He *could* use alcohol or drugs to escape, or bury himself in a book or a television program, or in a fight with his wife or kids. Because he can review his self-talk, however, his specific self put-downs can be recognized. Generalizations can be identified and thought through. Self-derogatory statements can be checked with others. The self-talk can serve as the basis for further learning and personal growth. To some extent, self-destructive thoughts can be refuted and eliminated.

The group leader's self-disclosure seems to clarify the requirements for several group members, but not for Steve, who simply cannot understand that he is leaving out a vital step. Those who do understand try, almost desperately, to lead Steve to meet the competency. Eventually, a counselor points out that it is beginning to seem as if several people are trying to give Steve the answer, and that the real work for Steve is to find his own answers.

As group closes, several members seem contemplative, some having expressed a desire to fit their new understanding of the competencies into their own self-knowledge. Others are obviously still bewildered and upset. Steve seems worn-out and somewhat sullen and stubborn. He states that he is still certain that he understands the competencies and has met them.

When the group meets the following week, Steve announces that he wishes to complete his evaluation. He states that, in the previous session, everyone gave him a lot of support. He does *not* mention that the group leaders gave him nonsupportive feedback. He minimizes his difficulties. Three members who were absent the previous week give him supportive feedback. Then Jim asks Steve to deal again with the process he goes through when he wants to drink. Jim sounds angry once again. "I thought what you said was just fine, but they (the leaders) told us it was wrong!" There follows, essentially, a repeat of the previous week's session. Steve ignores Jim's emotional state. He is again unable to demonstrate awareness of *specific* thoughts which he has about himself which lead to feelings, described generally and non-specifically as "inferiority.'' As he talks, Steve looks at the floor, takes surreptitious glances at the leaders, and does not disclose his feelings, in the present, at all. Once again, members who have begun to understand the competencies try to help Steve. Unfortunately, Steve has resorted to old ways and does not seem to have his newly learned behaviors available to help him through this stressful situation. A second meeting passes, slowly and painfully, and Steve never asks others to support a consensus decision for him to leave the group. At the next meeting another member begins an evaluation with no comment from or about Steve. As weeks pass, however, the learning that occurred in these two sessions is often observable in the changed behaviors of Steve and other group members.

An individual whose termination is supported by the entire group behaves quite differently from Steve. Throughout the evaluation s/he self-discloses, deals with what is happening in the present, and keeps the group focus on present reality. The client demonstrates a specific knowledge of his/her self-talk and self-defeating process and shows the group that that process can now be interrupted and changed. In short, the terminating group member has learned to use the behavioral competencies skillfully and effectively to meet his/her needs.

THE COUNSELOR

Most counselor input is designed to bring into focus the behaviors demonstrated in the group. It is the counselor's responsibility to foster self-disclosure and to encourage group members to deal with their feelings in the present. Leaders avoid making value judgments, commenting instead on reactions to specific behaviors, thereby modelling the giving of feedback.

The importance of a co-leader should not be underestimated. Many aspects of group behavior are related to the perceived difference in status between leaders and group members. If such issues are dealt with and processed, they can be a source of learning for the entire group. The level of leader involvement with group members may have an effect on the objectivity necessary for optimal learning. Resistance, attacks on leadership, and points at which leaders become "stuck" may serve to block the group. At such times, the co-leader performs an important function. S/he has a perspective resulting from greater distance and can often make a process comment about what is happening in the group. Often the co-leader can conceptualize occurrences in terms which highlight behaviors with which a client gets him/herself in trouble. Such process comments and conceptualizations afford an excellent backdrop against which group members can evaluate their behaviors.

Group members are encouraged to take over counselor activities and to become leaders in the group. Since it is necessary for the group members to become active in this process, it is important that leaders not usurp their opportunities to do their own work. Leaders who are too quick to give feedback, make process comments or answer questions deprive group members of the opportunity to demonstrate leadership behaviors. Both the number and the content of counselor statements are important. Often a dilemma is experienced. The group behaves as though no member knows how to meet competencies. At such times it may be necessary to suffer through long periods when the entire group is not focusing on the assigned task. By so doing, the leaders perform a most important function. They do not "rescue" the troubled group member. By refusing to provide answers or indicate ways in which the struggling individual might take care of him/herself, the counselors force the dependent member to assume responsibility.

Rescuers often emerge from the group membership at these times, offering advice as to how a problem might be handled. Such advice seems, usually, to provide the passive member with an opportunity to further rationalize his/her inability to act. The well-meaning helper then experiences frustration and anger, because the *rescuer's* needs are not being met. The attempted rescue may result in a situation in which the "stubborn" or "stupid" group member is punished for failure to act as instructed. The member seeking help will then, naturally, regard the process as unhelpful and will be tempted to withdraw. It may be useful, at this point, for a leader to self-disclose feelings of anxiety, frustration, and anger, and to tie them in to the process taking place. Nurturant comments, expressing understanding toward those involved, can also be effective in promoting learning and changing the tone of the group.

The counselor chooses the time for and the type of intervention to be made. Whether s/he chooses to focus on the process occurring in the group, on modeling appropriate behaviors, or on suggesting experiments for individual group members, there are an infinite variety of interventions available. The ultimate choice depends on that aspect of the situation which the counselor decides to make "figure." This depends upon the counselor's experience, values, ability to make connections between behaviors and ability to be accepting of self and others. In a very real sense, it is the counselor's awareness of him/herself which serves as a source for feedback.

Group leaders and experienced group members often focus on nonverbal aspects of a member's behavior. Movements indicating boredom, avoidance of individual contact, the presence of anger, fear, joy or caring are all grist for the group mill. All can be processed by the group and may supply valuable learning. All may be used in the feedback process to increase individual and group awareness.

Language usage is an important source of information and is basic to the process of cognitive restructuring. Use of pronouns which allow the individual to obscure issues of responsibility are discouraged. For example, "It makes you feel bad when . . . " or "we feel bad when . . . " can be transformed to "I feel discouraged when . . . " This is meaningful self-disclosure—a statement of thoughts and feelings. The pronoun is changed to "I," demonstrating the speaker's ownership of the (specific) feeling of discouragement. Focus on such verbal behavior provides learning for the entire group.

Creative Interventions counselors teach clients to distinguish between thoughts and feelings. Unfortunately, English (mis)usage has helped to blur the boundaries between the two distinctly separate processes. Any time the statement "I feel" is followed by the preposition "that," a thought, and not a feeling, is being expressed. In order for a feeling to be expressed, the verb "feel" must be followed immediately by a feeling word. A simple test as to whether or not a feeling is being expressed is to ask the question, "Could I change the statement to 'I am . . . ?'" In other words, "I feel that you are not listening to me," is a thought. A feeling statement would be, "I feel hurt because I think you aren't listening to me." Or, "I am hurt because you aren't listening to me." This may appear simple. In reality, it is often difficult for clients to understand the relationship of their feelings to their thoughts.

That feelings are the result of (controllable) thoughts is, therefore, clarified. The statement that the speaker feels "bad," a vague and generalized description of an emotional state, can be changed and the feeling specified as "discouraged." This makes it possible to examine the thought processes which result in the feeling of discouragement. Assumptions and faulty thought processes can then be challenged and modified. Once the thoughts have been identified, the present orientation of the group allows the group members to check on the validity of their assumptions and the appropriateness of their thoughts. Feedback is invaluable in this process. Incongruencies, and irrelevant and irresponsible statements, when identified, serve as important sources of learning for all.

Counselor may choose to limit their interventions giving clients ample opportunity to do their own work. Leader feedback to clients during evaluations is generally left till last. If the leader has noticed issues with which the group is not dealing, feedback may be withheld and a process comment made instead. By making process comments, the leader may heighten awareness of the avoidance of important issues, feelings, and present reality. Because this is precisely how group members fail to take care of themselves, it is a key element in alcohol misuse problems. For example, in an evaluation, a client received a great deal of support. Most feedback, however, contained clearly dissonant elements:

> You're doing real good. I'd say you meet all the competencies on a regular basis. I remember the last time you had an evaluation, and you got feedback that you should be more assertive. Since then, I see you really being more assertive. Except, not for the past couple of weeks, and I'm a little worried about that. But I've seen you do it lots of times, and I know you can, and I'd support a consensus for you to leave.

There are a number of questionable points in this statement. There are no specific behaviors relating to competencies mentioned. The person making these remarks confuses feedback with advice. The message contains conflicting statements and clearly indicates that the evaluee does *not* demonstrate specific assertive behaviors on a regular basis. The statement "I'd support a consensus," could be a demonstration of irresponsible behavior. A group consensus is an agreement among members. Each member must decide what decision is palatable, unpopular though that decision may be. To express reservations but leave the decision making process to others is a clear avoidance of responsible behavior.

Observing this process, the leader may decide to make a general or a specific process comment. A general comment might be:

"There seems to be something going on in this group. I'm not quite sure what it is, but I think there are some issues which are not being dealt with. I would rather wait to give my feedback and stay with the process a little longer." Such a comment gives group members ample opportunity to reflect on what has been occurring and to deal with it in an appropriate manner. A more specific process comment might be:

I've noticed something happening in this group which worries me. Many comments have made it clear that Bob does not meet the competencies regularly. The feedback has been rather vague, and I doubt if it has been very helpful to Bob. I've noticed, too, that many members have admitted to having reservations about Bob's meeting the competencies and, yet, you all are willing to let Bob through. I am worried. I do not think you, as group members, are behaving responsibly. You seem to be wanting to be nice to Bob, and *I* think you are letting him go before he may be ready. Possibly, you are meeting your needs instead of Bob's. And, Bob, I want you to know that I think that, if you were ready to leave, it would be you—not me—making these comments.

While this comment has the advantage of alerting group members to an important process which is taking place, it has the disadvantage of possible misinterpretation. Process comments can be experienced as threats and rejections and members, particularly new members, may withdraw and/or find it more difficult to participate actively.

It is important for group leaders to make both general and specific process comments. General comments allow group members to make their own interpretations about what is occurring. Specific process comments demonstrate thought processes which may be used to make helpful changes in the group. The importance of thoughtfully executed process comments should not be underestimated.

Many of the difficulties which are encountered in clients' lives are associated with the inability to deal adequately with figures of authority. Fortunately, the group leader is such a figure. Dependent group members may display counterdependent or overdependent behaviors. Counterdependent behaviors are often displayed as criticism of leaders, of group rules, and of the competencies.

Over-dependent members may be anxious to please leaders, asking for much direction and checking for cues as to whether or not leaders are pleased. Such members seem to need rules and regulations in this ambiguous experience.

Opposition to the leader, clearly and appropriately expressed, may be regarded as a sign of health. Such behavior involves the taking of risks and the demonstration of assertiveness. Group leaders who react defensively to group members' independence are generally counterproductive. Clients respond with increased passivity. The leaders' acceptance and encouragement of nonsupportive feedback from group members actually promotes responsible client behavior.

Group silence is useful, providing time for valuable thought as well as opportunity for the performance of constructive behaviors. Statements such as "I hate these silences—nothing ever happens in this group. We waste too much time!" clearly indicate that needs are not being met. Just as clearly the group members who make these statements do not accept responsibility for their own learning. Silences are welcomed by leaders as they offer opportunities for experimentation and for the assumption of leadership roles by group members.

The counselors' primary functions are associated with helping group members to demonstrate the eleven competencies. When members have difficulty with competencies, it may be necessary for the counselor to model them. More valuable, however, is modeling by other members, some of whom may have been in the group for a considerable period of time. The revolving membership of the group is helpful here. Changes observed in older group members provide inspiration and motivation for others. It is the job of the counselor to allow space and time for members to experiment with assertive leadership behaviors.

SUMMARY

Model reinforcement counseling, cognitive restructuring, and a gestalt orientation are seen as essential elements in the Creative Interventions' program. These theoretical foundations provide the basis for a growth-producing process which promotes the formation of responsible decisions and behaviors.

The difficult problem associated with measurement of program effectiveness has been incorporated into the learning process with the inclusion of peer evaluation and a list of observable behavioral competencies. These competencies help the group members to become aware of individual responsibility and power in interpersonal situations. The accomplishment of individual objectives through the practice of the competencies reinforces their performance and provides group leaders with a sound basis for evaluation of performance. Individuals who have demonstrated the competencies on a regular basis, and have been seen by the group membership as doing so, are able to receive, through a process of group consensus, support from the entire membership for a decision that they may leave the group experience. A low rate of recidivism (less than 1% rearrests) seems to attest to the effectiveness of such an approach.

REFERENCES

American Psychiatric Association. *Diagnostic and statistical manual of mental disorders* (3rd ed.). Washington, D.C.: American Psychiatric Association, 1980.

Appleton, G.M., and Katz, J. Creative interventions in an alcohol awareness program. *Pretrial Services Annual Journal*, September 1982, *5*: 102–115.

Bandura, A. *Social learning theory.* Englewood Cliffs, N.J.: Prentice Hall, 1977.

Beck, A.T., Rush, A.J., Shaw, B.F., & Emery, G. *Cognitive therapy of depression.* New York: Guilford Press, 1979.

Emery, G. Self-reliance training in depression. In D.P. Rathjen & J.P. Foreyt (Eds.), *Social competence: interventions for children and adults.* New York: Pergamon Press, 1980.

Fillmore, K.M., & Midanik, L. Chronicity of drinking problems among men: a longitudinal study. *Journal of Studies on Alcohol*, *45*: 228–236, 1984.

Peele, Stanton. The cultural context of psychological approaches to alcoholism: Can we control the effects of alcohol? *American Psychologist*, December 1984, *39*, No. 12, 1337–1351.

Perls, F., Hefferline, R.F., & Goodman, P. *Gestalt therapy.* New York: Crown Publishers, 1951.

Polster, E., & Polster, M. *Gestalt therapy integrated: contours of theory and practice.* New York: Random House, 1973.

Rotheram, M.J. Social skills training program in elementary and high school classrooms. In D.P. Rathjen & J.P. Foreyt (Eds.), *Social competence: interventions for children and adults.* New York: Pergamon Press, 1980.

Steiner, C.M. *Healing alcoholism.* New York: Grove Press, 1979.

Valerio, A.M., Kane, K., & Saiger, F.S. DWI diversion in Monroe County: the role of Pre-Trial Diversion. *Pretrial Services Annual Journal*, September 1982, *5*: 94–101.

Operating Under the Influence: Programs and Treatment for Convicted Offenders in Massachusetts

Michael V. Fair

ABSTRACT. Massachusetts legislation passed in September 1982, increased the penalties for operating under the influence of alcohol (OUI) and was followed by a dramatic change in the processing of drunk driving offenses. This article examines what is currently available and proposed in terms of programs and facilities for individuals convicted of operating under the influence in Massachusetts and presents suggestions concerning the further development of programs. The information was collected in a series of semi-structured interviews with representatives from Massachusetts agencies and institutions providing programs and/or custody for the OUI population.

INTRODUCTION

In 1982 the Massachusetts General Court passed legislation (M.G.L. Chapter 373) which increased the certainty of punishment and stiffened the penalties for the offense of "operating a motor vehicle while under the influence of intoxicating liquors" (OUI). The new law, effective September 1, 1982, increased the fines imposed for drunk driving, established mandatory license suspension, and included provisions for minimum terms of imprisonment, especially for repeat offenders.

The penalties for driving while intoxicated correspond roughly to the number of prior convictions for that offense. Along with a minimum fine of $100 and loss of license for a year, first offenders are subject to a period of probation supervision or a maximum of two years imprisonment. Second offenders are assessed a fine of $300,

Michael V. Fair is Commissioner of Correction for the Commonwealth of Massachusetts.
The author wishes to acknowledge and thank Ms. Kathleen Moore and Ms. Mariellen Fidrych for their assistance in preparing this article.

89

lose their license for two years, and can be incarcerated for seven days if they do not choose to participate in a 14-day residential alcohol treatment program. Multiple offenders or individuals assigned to an alcohol program two or more times in the preceding six years are fined a minimum of $500, lose their license for five years, and must serve a term of imprisonment of at least 60 days but not more than two years. In addition to the more stringent penalties for drunk driving, the new law incorporates provisions for alcohol education and treatment. Attention to alcohol programming is reflected particularly in the sentencing guidelines for first and second offenders.

Two independent reports have indicated that the new law has resulted in substantial changes in the processing of OUI cases. The Office of Probation reported that guilty findings for OUI offenses increased 245 percent from 1981 to the spring of 1983 (Brown, Argeriou and McCarty, 1984). The Department of Correction found that commitments to county facilities for operating under the influence increased by 173 percent during the first sixteen months after the enactment of the new law (Williams, 1984). These two studies suggest that the OUI population has had a tremendous impact on the criminal justice system within a short period of time.

Given the changes brought about by the passage of Chapter 373, a question arises as to whether existing facilities and programs can adequately accommodate the influx of this new offender population. This article examines the programs and treatment which now exist and are proposed for the sentenced OUI population. Particular emphasis is placed on the range of services and programs available to the multiple OUI offender and the kinds of problems encountered in meeting the needs of the repeat offender population.

Chapter 373 of the Acts of 1982 targets first offenders, second offenders and multiple offenders for different types of penalties and treatment in order to deter further drinking and driving. Court dispositions for the first 10 months of 1984 indicate that while the vast majority of offenders (63 percent) processed under Chapter 373 were required to attend Driver Alcohol Education classes, a significant number were placed in a residential alcohol treatment program and/or incarcerated (see Table 1). This article focuses primarily on the programs established and envisioned for the latter groups, the repeat offenders.[1] (See Figure 1.)

---

[1]This research was conducted under the supervision of Linda Holt and Larry Williams, DOC Research Unit. Research staff revised and edited the final draft of this report.

Table 1

Court Dispositions of OUI Cases Heard
between January and October, 1984

Dispositions	Cases	Percent
Not Guilty	1,478	(5)
Driver's Alcohol Education (24-D)	18,296	(63)
Residential Alcohol Treatment	3,574	(12)
Residential Treatment/Jail	482	(2)
Incarceration	984	(3)
Other (Probation/Fines)	4,097	(14)
Total	28,911	(100)

Source: Memorandum from Linda Druker, Manager of Research,
Office of Probation, December, 21, 1984.

Figure 1

The conditions of Sentence by
OUI Offense History

SENTENCE CONDITIONS	FIRST	SECOND	THIRD OR SUBSEQUENT
Minimum Fine	$100	$300	$500
Revocation of License	1 year	2 years	5 years
Reduced License Revocation	30 days if attending DAEP*	1 year if special hearing	2 years if special hearing
Minimum Terms of Incarceration	none	7 days or 14 days in Residential Treatment	60 days

*DAEP: Driver Alcohol Education Program

FINDINGS

Figure 1 presents a summary of the sentence conditions established by Chapter 373 for the offense of operating under the
influence.

First-Offender Program: Alcohol Education

Individuals convicted of operating under the influence for the
first time may be incarcerated up to 2 years, but it is not usual for

a judge to sentence them to jail. Generally the offender receives a term of supervised probation and must participate in the Driver Alcohol Education Program (DAEP). These educational programs are operated by the Division of Alcoholism, under the auspices of the Department of Public Health. There are 29 programs throughout the state which provide eight weeks of alcohol education and counseling. A fee of $280 from each participant covers three diagnostic interviews and eight classes.

According to the Department of Public Health the Driver Alcohol Education Program served approximately 25,258 clients between July 1, 1983 and June 30, 1984. In the DAEP, clients are given information about alcohol use and abuse, made aware of the dangers of drinking and driving, and encouraged to assess and change their drinking behavior.The DAEP also screens clients, assesses their alcohol problems, and recommends treatment. The evaluations are shared with clients. Sixty percent of the clients in the Driver Alcohol Education Program are referred to additional treatment programs. There are eighty treatment programs throughout the state which provide a variety of counseling services to alcohol abuses. The court is informed of the assessment, and a progress report is sent to the court shortly after completion of the program. After a client completes the diagnostic/educational component, aftercare management is provided to all clients for the duration of the probation period. The goals of aftercare management are to link the client to treatment services, to motivate the client to remain in care, and to monitor the client's progress for probation purposes.

Second-Offender Program: Residential Alcohol Treatment

Under Chapter 373, judges may place second offenders on probation instead of the minimum 7-day jail sentence provided that a condition of probation be confinement for no less than fourteen consecutive days in a residential treatment program. There are currently four such programs, the first of which is at Rutland Heights Hospital. These programs are aimed at addressing the alcohol-related problems of second-time offenders and reducing the overcrowding of county facilities. The Rutland Program opened on October 1982 with a capacity of 88 beds and expanded to 131 beds in February 1984. Participants pay a fee of $480 to cover the expense of treatment at Rutland.

Initially, few offenders were attending the Rutland Heights

Program. Courts were giving the second offenders the option of seven days in jail or fourteen days at Rutland. Offenders were opting for jail since the sentence was shorter and there was no fee of $480. During the summer of 1983 an intensive orientation regarding the residential treatment program was given to judges, prosecutors, probation officials, and parole officials. After this orientation, many courts started giving longer jail sentences making the Rutland Heights program more attractive. The consequence was a six-month waiting list of about 1,700 for the residential treatment program.

Approximately 2,416 clients were admitted to the program at Rutland Heights between July 1, 1983 and June 30, 1984. The Rutland program is similar to a minimum security institution. At every meeting there is a head count and clients may leave the building only with a pass or a staff member. When a client is admitted to the program, they are given a schedule to be followed for the two-week period. The schedule consists of recreation and a series of alcohol rehabilitation lectures on such topics as OUI laws, alcohol related diseases, Alcoholics Anonymous, and stress management. The clients each have a counselor who assesses their alcohol problem and develops an aftercare program. At the end of the fourteen days, the counselor sends a letter to the court which evaluates the client's progress in the program. Upon completion of the program at Rutland, the client attends an aftercare treatment program. The length of stay in aftercare treatment depends upon the degree and nature of the client's alcohol problem.

Programs replicating the Rutland Heights concept are presently operating at the following locations:

—Lakeville Hospital opened a 60 bed program in January 1985 for a total of 120 admissions per month. The program is administered by the Department of Public Health.
—Tewksbury State Hospital opened a 60 bed program in May 1985 for 120 admissions monthly. The program is administered by the Department of Public Health.
—Middlesex County Hospital opened a 60 bed program in April 1985 for 120 admissions monthly. The Middlesex program is administered by the Middlesex County Commissioner's office under contract with the Department of Public Health.

Additionally, new beds were added to the Rutland program in

January 1985 for a total of 151. Presently, the Rutland program can accommodate 302 second offenders monthly.

Multiple Offender Program: The County Correctional System

Under the new legislation, a third or subsequent offender must spend a minimum of 60 days in jail. While it is possible for individuals convicted of OUI for the first time to serve a jail sentence, it is more likely that the OUI offender sentenced to a term of imprisonment is a repeat offender who may already have been through a Driver Alcohol Education Program. Because the sentences for OUI offenses carry a minimum length of two years, the sentences are most often served in county houses of correction.

The OUI Offender in County Facilities

In 1983 OUI offenders represented about 25% of all admissions to county houses of correction (Williams, 1984). This proportion varied dramatically among the various counties. In Suffolk County only 7 percent of the commitments were for OUI; while in Middlesex, Essex, and Hampshire counties commitments for OUI accounted for 30, 33, and 35 percent, respectively, of all commitments (see Table 2). Thus, as the statistics suggest the impact of the OUI offender on the county facility varied considerably.

The county houses of correction handle almost exclusively a male population. Only Franklin County and Berkshire County currently have any facilities for female offenders. Most female offenders serve their sentences at the women's state prison, at MCI-Framingham. In 1983 ten percent ($N = 68$) of the commitments at MCI-Framingham were for OUI, an increase from two percent in 1980. Like other offense categories, only a very small proportion of the OUI population is female.

County officials generally agreed that the new drunk driving legislation has had the most noticeable impact on the house of correction inmate population rather than the county jail awaiting trial population. Driving under the influence was an offense for which individuals were often released on a pre-trial basis (Brown, Argeriou and McCarty, 1984).

Many of the county correctional officials interviewed mentioned differences they observed between the incarcerated OUI offender and the typical county inmate. However, these perceptions were not

Table 2

Commitments to County Correctional Facilities
in 1983 by Offense Type

	Operating Under The Influence		Other Offenses	
County	Number	Percent	Number	Percent
Middlesex	650	(35)	1213	(65)
Essex	361	(33)	719	(67)
Hampshire	73	(30)	169	(70)
Worcester	406	(26)	1165	(74)
Norfolk	170	(26)	480	(74)
Plymouth	139	(26)	404	(74)
Barnstable	81	(25)	240	(75)
Bristol	132	(20)	512	(80)
Berkshire	66	(18)	299	(82)
Hampden	188	(17)	911	(83)
Franklin	25	(15)	145	(85)
Dukes	12	(13)	81	(87)
Suffolk	69	(7)	907	(93)

Source: Williams, County Commitments for Driving Under the Influence
of Alcohol, 1984.

unanimous among the county authorities; some respondents saw
more similarities than differences between the two types of inmates.
The distinguishing factors stressed were (1) differences in background and social characteristics of the two types of inmates; (2) the
non-criminal nature of the OUI offender; and (3) the seriousness of
alcohol abuse among OUI offenders.

There was general agreement among the county correctional
authorities that the drunk driving offenders who went through their
facilities were repeat OUI offenders with serious alcohol abuse
problems. Few could be characterized as ''social drinkers'' exhibiting behaviors easily deterred by the threat of imprisonment.
Alcohol problems, reportedly, were so serious for some that their
sobriety lasted only as long as the period of incarceration. Chronic
alcohol abuse problems made detoxification a critical issue in
managing the OUI offender population. County correctional personnel reported using the medical units of their facilities for the

purposes of detoxification and monitoring of health problems associated with alcohol abuse.

County correctional officials identified a number of factors which they felt distinguished OUI offenders from other county inmates. They indicated that OUI offenders tended to be better educated, have more steady employment records, be more settled, and be older than typical county commitments. There is some empirical evidence to support these observations. A 1983 study by the Department of Correction (Williams, 1984) found that, in contrast to the general county population, the OUI population was older, more educated, and more likely to be married. Generally, it was concluded that the OUI population presented less of a security problem than the rest of the county correctional population.

The county interviews also revealed that there was a lack of concensus on whether or not the OUI population could be considered "non-criminal" or different from the typical property and violent offenders found in the county correctional system. Those who argued that OUI offenders were atypical maintained that: (1) their criminal history was usually limited to traffic or alcohol-related offenses; (2) most were experiencing their first incarceration; and (3) the offense itself stemmed from an alcohol problem better handled through treatment than incarceration. County officials also felt that because of age differences and limited prison experience, most OUI offenders would undergo unusual difficulties adjusting to the youthful inmate culture found in many county facilities.

Other county authorities expressed the opinion that OUI offenders were much like other county commitments. In many cases, county offenders may be charged with a number of crimes including driving under the influence, but committed for just one of the offenses. Because of plea bargaining the committing offense may not always be the most serious offense. For example, an individual may be charged with operating under the influence and operating after revocation of a license but be committed on the revocation charge. Similarly, an individual charged with motor vehicle theft and operating under the influence could, on the basis of plea bargaining, be sentenced only for the OUI offense. To the extent that these sentencing outcomes are widespread, the OUI population in the county correctional system may not be as distinct as some believe.

Existing Programs in County Facilities

Most counties offer alcohol-related programs to the general offender population that are also available to OUI offenders. Some county correctional facilities have developed specialized treatment programs and segregated housing targeted specifically for the OUI population. Figure 2 summarizes the types of programming reportedly available to OUI offenders in each of the county's correctional facilities.

The most common program available to the OUI offender was Alcoholics Anonymous (AA). This program usually met two or three times a week in the institution and was open to all inmates in a facility. AA was generally run by persons from the community and depended upon voluntary attendance by inmates. Alcoholics Anonymous was available to county inmates in all counties except Suffolk. It should be noted that Suffolk county officials reported no alcohol programming, whatever, either for the OUI population or the general inmate population. Moreover, three counties—Franklin, Hampshire, and Norfolk—offered no special alcohol programs other than AA. Together these four counties received approximately 14 percent of the OUI commitments in 1983, although the proportions in the county correctional populations which were OUI offenders ranged from a low of seven percent in Suffolk to a high of 30 percent in Hampshire (refer to Table 2).

MCI-Framingham has a number of alcohol and substance abuse programs available for OUI as well as other offenders. Al-Anon is a support group for individuals who have been affected by the alcoholism of a family member or another close associate and meets weekly within the institution. SPAN, Inc. is a substance abuse program for individuals with drug or alcohol problems. This is a program for individuals within 12 months of release and provides weekly counseling programs in group and individual sessions. Finally, Sobriety Program for the Rehabilitation of Inmates with New Goals (SPRING) provides daily group or individual counseling for inmates with drug or alcohol problems.

Most county officials stressed the importance of involving OUI offenders in a variety of "re-entry" programs during their incarceration. Re-entry programs attempt to link the offender to community services so that program participation can continue after release from prison. Re-entry programs generally try to connect offenders

Figure 2

Existing Programs Available to OUI Offenders
in County Correctional Facilities

County Correctional System	AA	Alcohol Counseling	Other Alcohol Programs	Re-Entry Program	Minimum Security	Community-Based Programs
Barnstable	X	X				
Berkshire	X		X			X
Bristol	X	X	X	X		
Dukes	X		X			
Essex	X	X	X	X	X	
Franklin	X					
Hampden	X	X	X	X	X	X
Middlesex	X				X	
Norfolk	X					
Plymouth	X	X		X		
Suffolk						
Worcester	X	X	X		X	
MCI-Framingham	X	X	X	X		

with a variety of education, employment, and alcohol abuse services in the community.

Many of the county correctional systems try to establish relationships with programs operating in the community. In some cases participation can begin while the offender is in the institution and continue after the offender is released. In particular, Hampden and Berkshire Counties have developed active relationships with community-based alcohol programs that supplement programs run by the institutions and provide follow-through in the community. Some county officials indicated that ties with community-based services were difficult to establish because community programs and halfway houses were reluctant to accept referrals from correctional facilities.

Most correctional officials agreed that minimum security settings were appropriate for the majority of OUI offenders. However, many of the county facilities only have higher security areas and therefore are not able to move OUI offenders to lower security. Those counties that do have lower security housing areas use them extensively for the OUI population.

Most county officials did not believe that OUI offenders presented a security problem. Most had provisions for returning the OUI offender to general population in a secure area if there were disciplinary problems. Middlesex County specifically mentioned this provision for managing OUI offenders with disciplinary problems. One county official cautioned that the lack of supervision in some minimum security programs such as home furloughs could encourage the resumption of problematic drinking behavior.

While most county officials agreed that lower security was the most appropriate placement for the OUI population, space constraints and policies regarding new arrivals and those with short sentences often result in the placement of OUI offenders in very secure environments. For example, in Suffolk County all offenders are placed in a new man section for the first 30 days where they are locked up for 23 hours a day. The result of this policy in Suffolk institutions is that most OUI offenders spend their entire incarceration in very secure environments.

Issues in management of the OUI population. Many of the county officials indicated the presence of unique problems the correctional facilities encountered when dealing with the OUI population. Most of these management problems stemmed from the sentence conditions and special needs of the OUI offender.

Perhaps the most commonly mentioned problem was sentence length. Many of the OUI offenders have short sentences of seven days, and many have sentences that are only to be served on weekends. In 1983, 1,304 (55 percent) of the OUI offenders committed to county correctional facilities had sentences of less than one month, 965 (41 percent) had sentences of 7 days or less, and another three percent (73 offenders) were fined but might have served time in jail if unable to pay the fines (Williams, 1984). County officials find it difficult to develop effective programs for short stays. Weekend sentences pose the additional problem of occurring when treatment staff are off duty. Booking, classification, and orientation may take several days to several weeks to complete; consequently, it is not unusual for OUI offenders to have served their sentence before a treatment plan can be developed or they become eligible for general programming. "Re-entry" programming becomes critical for this short-term population.

On a weekend sentence offenders serve their period of imprisonment over the course of several weekends. Originally this type of sentencing was intended to benefit both offenders and correctional personnel. Weekend sentencing was supposed to help correctional staff deal with crowded institutions and, at the same time, allow offenders to maintain their employment. However, correctional officials found weekend sentences caused a number of management problems. It increased the paperwork associated with admissions and releases at a time when correctional staff was already reduced. Contraband became a problem because other inmates would ask weekenders to smuggle prohibited goods into the institution for them. Even though weekenders might actually avoid transporting the contraband, they felt intimidated by the requests. Finally, the need for detoxification increased because weekenders with serious alcohol problems would relapse into their former habits when on leave. Frequent detoxification taxed resources of correctional facilities.

Several correctional authorities mentioned the lack of adequate resources as an obstacle to the development of improved correctional programming for the OUI population. Many are working in institutions that are old, overcrowded, under court order to depopulate, and lacking resources for programs for even the general offender population. Under these conditions the correctional experience becomes purely punitive offering little in the way of rehabilitation for the OUI offender.

RECOMMENDATIONS FOR PROGRAM DEVELOPMENT

There was little consensus about the most effective type of treatment for the OUI offender. Some felt that small group or individual professional counseling was the best type of programming, while others felt that self-help groups like AA were the most useful in dealing with these offenders.

Some counties mentioned the need for more medically oriented services including increased availability of detoxification centers and the possibility of using hospitals rather than houses of correction for the purposes of treatment of the OUI offender. Others mentioned the need for increased awareness regarding the issues of problem drinking. This could be done by more community education programs so that individuals could recognize alcohol in themselves or others before it resulted in an OUI commitment.

Most of the county correctional authorities supported the establishment of special regional facilities to house and provide supervision for repeat OUI offenders. However, some of the remote counties (Berkshire and Dukes, for example) did not feel that a regional facility would have much impact on their systems. Those that argue in favor of regional correctional facilities for drunk drivers suggested that the OUI problem was really a state problem rather than a county problem. It is not unusual for drunk drivers to be arrested in counties that are contiguous to their residence. This is the case in Norfolk county where it is common for Suffolk County residents to be arrested for driving under the influence. Since Suffolk County does not receive an equal share of OUI offenders, the custody of OUI offenders creates an undue burden on Norfolk's correctional resources. Regional facilities would enable county correctional systems to ease overcrowding by accepting one segment of their popoulation and freeing up needed space for the remainder of the county offender population.

Specialized Regional Facilities for OUI Offenders

As a response to overcrowding and treatment issues related to the OUI offender population, the Governor's anti-crime council recommended the establishment of three regional centers located in Western Massachusetts, Southeastern Massachusetts, and Metropolitan Boston, to house approximately 125 OUI offenders at each.

The first of these facilities opened in March 1985 and is administered by the Massachusetts Department of Correction. The Longwood Treatment Center focuses its primary mission on the provision of comprehensive program services for the alcoholic offender. Residents admitted to Longwood are third or multiple OUI offenders who are committed to a county house of correction and are screened to eligibility and suitability to participate in the treatment program. Individuals with a history of prior incarceration in state or federal facilities for a violent offense would not be eligible for placement. Moreover, individuals with weekend or holiday sentences would not be eligible for placement.

Longwood Treatment Center is a minimum security facility oriented to alcohol treatment and recovery. Individual treatment plans are developed for each resident which include participation in alcohol education classes, Alcoholics Anonymous, individual and group counseling, and aftercare planning. An important part of the programming is the involvement of the offender's family when possible in counseling sessions. Additionally, residents are monitored upon their discharge from Longwood in order to assess their recovery process and status.

Thus far, Longwood Treatment Center has served to benefit both offenders and county correctional facilities. The benefits to the offender consist of a more extensive and specialized treatment in a lower security environment than many counties can provide. The benefits to the county correctional system consist of some relief in the overcrowding of facilities and a transfer of costs for these offenders from the counties to the state. It is anticipated that the regional centers in western and southeastern Massachusetts will be equally beneficial in serving this unique population.

REFERENCES

Blacker, Edward, Ph.D., *Directory of Division of Alcoholism Approved Treatment and Intervention Programs for OUI Offenders Subsequent to Driver Alcohol Educational Programs*, Department of Public Health, Division of Alcoholism, Boston.

Brown, Marjorie E., Milton Ageriou, Ph.D. and Dennis McCarty, Ph.D., *An Evaluation of Drunk Driving in Massachusetts Under Chapter 373, Acts of 1982*, (a joint research project between the Office of Probation and The Division of Alcoholism), Massachusetts Trial Court, August 1, 1984.

Massachusetts Senate Committee on Post Audit and Oversight, *Drinking and Driving in Massachusetts*, Boston, 1982.

Williams, Lawrence T., *County Commitments for Driving Under the Influence of Alcohol 1976 to 1983*, Massachusetts Department of Correction, Boston, 1984.

A Comprehensive Culturally Specific Approach to Drunk Driving for Blacks

Maxine Womble, M.A.
C. Vincent Bakeman, M.Ed., M.P.A., Ph.D.

ABSTRACT. In recent years, drunk driving has become a major public issue, primarily due to concerned citizen groups who have been involved in activities to increase public awareness about the pervasiveness of this problem. This article describes the national campaign by the National Black Alcoholism Council (NBAC) to establish a *Blacks Against Drunk Driving* (BADD) initiative. The approach recommended is from a Black Cultural Perspective that includes education and training for key staff in the criminal justice system who work with persons arrested for driving while intoxicated (DWI). There are also steps outlined to engage the Black community in the drunk driving campaign through "community education networking conferences."

INTRODUCTION

In recent years, there has been an increased amount of attention given to the devastating effects of drunk driving on the citizenry in this country. The elevation of this problem as a health issue is primarily due to the outcry from concerned citizen groups who have demanded that the federal and state government officials take steps to address this problem. As a result, more laws have been passed and programs implemented in numerous states that would lead to the reduction of drunk driving. This is not a new problem, but one that has existed since the appearance of the first automobile. The *Quarterly Journal of Inebriety* in 1904 (DOT, 1985) reported on a

---

Maxine Womble is Chairperson of the National Black Alcoholism Council, and President of Womble & Associates.

C. Vincent Bakeman is Chairperson of the National Black Alcoholism Council's Public Policy Committee, and Professor of Human Services at Kennedy-King College.

study of fatal crashes involving the "automobile Wagons." The
Editorial made an observation that:

> Inebriates and moderate drinkers are the most incapable of
> all persons to drive motor wagons. The general palsy and
> diminished power of control of both the reason and the senses
> are certain to invite disaster in every attempt to guide such
> wagons. (DOT, p. 3)

The presence of alcohol in highway accidents has escalated far
beyond anyone's expectation since 1904. Analysis of alcohol-
related accidents by Fells (1982) found that 24,000 to 27,500 people
were fatally injured in accidents between 1979 and 1980, which
represents 55 percent of all vehicle accidents. Data are not available
on the number of Black persons involved in fatal accidents.

The data collected nationally on drinking drivers by the Fatal
Accident Reporting System (FARS) of the National Highway
Traffic Safety Administration, and the National Accident Summary
System (NASS) must rely on the data submitted by local and state
bodies on accidents that occur on the nation's highways. One of the
deficiencies in the NASS and FARS data collection systems is the
absence of information on *race, ethnicity,* and the *socio-economic
status* of persons involved in traffic/highway accidents. Therefore,
studies utilizing data from these two systems also fail to include
valid national information about the involvement of Black or other
racial and ethnic groups in alcohol-related vehicle accidents. A
study by Zylman (1972), for example, only made reference to the
effect that increased alcohol involvement by non-whites is explained
as a socio-economic rather than racial effect, while other studies
found no conclusive evidence to support the assumption that low
income persons are more involved in drinking driving accidents.
Since the lack of uniformity in reporting accidents in each state
precludes accurate documentation of drunk driving accidents, some
caution must be exercised in accepting and utilizing the data
retrieved from the FARS and NASS systems.

Characteristics of Drunk Drivers

Research shows that men drive more frequently than women,
especially after drinking, and are therefore exposed to more alcohol-
related accidents (DOT, p. 28). This practice is also present among

Blacks. Harper (1981) noted that compared to Black women, a much larger proportion of Black men drive motor vehicles and work on dangerous industrial jobs. These are situations where accidents can easily occur to one under the influence of alcohol. In a study by Hyman (1968) that was designed to determine whether drivers involved in accidents were more often intoxicated than control drivers, he found that Black men showed blood alcohol levels above .10 percent five times as frequently as White men.

In looking at the age of persons involved in car accidents, teenage drivers have consistently had a higher accident involvement rate than the average driver. Motor accidents are the leading cause of death among young people 15 to 24 years old (NIAAA, 1982). Although Black youth are believed to be proportionately represented in fatal vehicle accidents, the consequences are far more detrimental if we look at the other life threatening problems that are also impacting on this age group. Research indicates that alcohol or drugs are involved in more than 50 percent of the murder cases in the Black community. The three top causes of death for Black men 15 to 24 were found to be accidents, suicide, and homicide (Gary, 1981). Since the median age for Black people in 1984 was 26.3 (U.S. Bureau of the Census) the implications are very serious for the Black population with this significantly high rate of males being killed each year who fall below the median age. There is cause to be concerned about the future stability of the Black family if this pattern continues.

Harper (1976, p. 41) points out that the patterns of alcohol use are often influenced by one's social class and that more public drinking (street corner gangs) and heavy weekend drivers will be found in the lower class, while middle-class Blacks will often drink in the privacy of their homes and clubs. Blacks tend to drink more on weekends and holidays. If data were available regarding national drinking and driving according to race, there would probably be evidence to support our theory that there is a higher rate of alcohol-related accidents among Blacks on weekends.

NBAC's Policy on Drunk Driving

Given the devastating consequences that drunk driving has on a proportionate number of Blacks who are killed or injured in alcohol-related vehicle accidents, it is incumbent upon all groups to become more involved in activities that would lead to the reduction of this crisis. Over the past 5 years numerous organizations were formed to increase the public's awareness about drunk driving. Such organizations like Mothers Against Drunk Drivers (MADD), Students Against Driving Drunk (SADD), and Physicians Against Drunk Driving (PADD), have been instrumental in stimulating state and federal legislation designed to reduce the rate of DWI accidents, but none of them have focused on the Black community. This was recognized by the National Black Alcoholism Council (NBAC) as a national unmet need.

NBAC, the only national organization specifically formed to address the concerns and issues related to alcohol abuse and alcoholism among Black people, initiated a drunk driving campaign targeted to the Black community in 1983. This effort is known as *Blacks Against Drunk Driving* (BADD).

The BADD program was developed under the leadership of the Vice Chairperson of NBAC, Dr. Frances Brisbane, and NBAC's Public Policy Committee, chaired by Dr. C. Vincent Bakeman. They were charged with the responsibility of developing the organization's public policy statement on drunk driving and establishing a program that would engage various NBAC State Chapters and organizations in the Black community in this national campaign.

The long range goal of the BADD campaign is to reduce the incidence of drunk driving among the Black population in general and to specifically focus on Black youth 15 to 24 years of age. Culturally-specific training and education will be provided for key personnel in the law enforcement and judicial system who are most likely to approach, arrest or provide other services for Black persons driving while intoxicated (DWI). The training and education programs were developed as a means to assist these key personnel to better understand the perspective from which most Blacks view law enforcement officials, and what must be done to overcome these barriers. The education and training should enhance their capabilities to relate more effectively with the Black drinking drivers and his/her significant other.

As a matter of public policy, NBAC

—Supports national, state and local government legislation which require all persons apprehended while driving under the influence of alcohol and other drugs, to participate in driver education programs specific to the dangers of driving and drinking.

—Promotes the establishment of a mandatory drinking and drug history report of all persons brought before the judicial system for acts of violence, including car accidents while intoxicated, spouse abuse, and homicide, in order to determine if alcohol/drug treatment, in addition to or instead of jail is needed.

—Encourages states to develop a driver education course, in which films are included, on the *Consequences of Driving While Alcohol and Drug Impaired*, and the attendance is mandatory for all applicants seeking a driver's license for the first time.

—Supports laws in which repeat offenders of driving while intoxicated receive mandatory suspension of driving privileges and are required to attend an extended period of alcoholism-specific treatment with successful completion as a condition for reinstatement of license.

—Encourages funding sources to require drunk and drugged driver education and prevention activities as part of all programs designed to treat teenagers.

—Encourages strong enforcement of dram shop laws and the education of parents and hosts of their potential liability in serving alcohol in their homes to already intoxicated individuals who subsequently injure someone while driving.

While there are differing views on how drunk drivers should be handled, ranging from the extremely punitive (let's incarcerate everyone), to the permissive (let's provide everyone with treatment). NBAC is not supportive of the punitive approach, that seeks to "lock them up and throw away the key," to imprison every DWI. NBAC's position is that steps should be taken to get drunk drivers off our highways and that every effort should be made to make appropriate interventions at all levels to reach the Black drinking driver and provide appropriate and just responses based on individualized assessments.

There is a conscious mistrust among Blacks about having any encounter with the "law." These feelings are deeply rooted because of past experiences with oppressive law enforcers. In view of these concerns, the BADD campaign focuses on some of the perceptions Black people have about the court system and police officers, and how Blacks are viewed by court and police personnel.

Court System: history tells us that Blacks who enter into the judicial system frequently do not always receive just sentences.

Justice too often is not blind when it comes to Blacks, in too many cases Blacks are given harsher sentences than Whites who commit the same offense. Whether this is due to poor legal representation, racism or insensitive court personnel, problems exist within the system that must be rectified. Based on reports from NBAC membership from around the country, Blacks arrested for drunk driving are frequently given harsher sentences by the courts than are Whites, and are seldom referred for appropriate assessments or to drunk driving remedial education and treatment programs by the courts.

Too often the court personnel cannot identify with Blacks that are brought before the courts and certain assumptions are made because they are in fact Black. In one situation where a Black female probation officer, accompanied by a police officer, brought a White probation violator into night court. The presiding judge made the assumption that the police officer had arrested the Black female and directed the police officer to bring her (the probation officer) before the bench. It is only natural that a Black would perceive this erroneous assumption made by the judge as an action predicated on racism and sexism.

NBAC's efforts must, therefore, involve activities that will educate and sensitize the principals employed in the court system about these concerns to increase better results for Black drunk drivers. It is also necessary to educate Blacks about laws that relate to the crime of drunk driving, and the various alternatives available in the formal and informal court system. An understanding of how blood, urine and breath alcohol analyses are used, and the options for assessments, education and treatment should be part of the educational process.

Police officers: there are some organizations and groups that strongly support stringent enforcement by police officers, including "safety checkpoints that involve the seizure of citizens in the absence of individualized suspicion that they have committed a violation." (DOT, 1983). Although the Supreme Court has ruled that an individual's rights under the Fourth Amendment are not violated by checkpoint stops for DWI enforcement *if* they are conducted in a *reasonable fashion* (DOT, p. 8). The problems will arise, however, if police are left to determine what is "reasonable." "Such matters cannot be left to the discretion of officers actually conducting the safety checkpoint" (p. 8).

The need for education and training for police officers is

extremely important if they are given the latitude to stop motorists without cause. The training should not only outline their responsibilities in terms of the law but also how Blacks will interpret being stopped by a police officer. Blacks tend to believe that they are arrested without cause at a higher rate than are Whites. These beliefs are supported by the findings by Larkins (1965) in his analysis of historical arrest documents. He found that Black male drinking offenders had been subject to discrimination in cases of Police arrest and court sentences. Zax et al. (1964) also found that twelve times as many Black men as White men were arrested for drunkenness during 1961 in the city of Rochester, New York. A study conducted by Hyman in Columbus, Ohio, found that there was an over-representation of Blacks among arrested drunk drivers.

Given these realities, it is necessary for steps to be taken by police departments to ensure that Blacks are not singled out and harassed if checkpoint stops, search of drivers and other such methods like these are used to deter drunk driving. Sensitivity training about how Blacks and police officers view each other, and techniques on how to approach Blacks when using the power of their positions should be part of the training that is supplemented with objective ongoing monitoring to help facilitate better communication and cooperation.

NBAC Approach to Drunk Driving

In addition to providing education and counseling services for key staff in the police and court systems, NBAC is actively engaged in activities that will promote increased understanding about the impact of drunk driving on the Black community. As Black people began to accept the devastating effects that alcohol abuse and alcoholism have on their families and their communities, and as they feel more comfortable and trusting of the treatment and judicial systems, more Blacks will become actively involved in the campaign to educate members of their own community about drunk driving and to encourage Blacks who are alcoholics or problem drinkers to seek treatment.

To increase the identification and referral of persons needing assistance for alcohol-related crimes will require some attitudinal changes by both Black and White people. Harvey (1985) points out that to Blacks it appears that the majority of society is more inclined to see White alcohol abusers as sick people who need to be referred for treatment, while Black alcohol abusers are treated by the establishment (especially but not exclusively the criminal justice component) as criminals. Hodges and Lowe (1977) found that the Black community inhibits intervention into the lives of Black alcoholics especially by White officials (police, social workers, public health nurses, etc.). In analyzing Blacks' tendency to protect the Black alcoholic, Harvey (1985) stated that

> It does not seem unreasonable that the members of an oppressed group would develop an ingroup understanding that certain levels of undesirable behavior would be tolerated in order to prevent sanctions and confinement being imposed on the offending community members by members of the ruling group. . . . The higher tolerance levels (Schiff, 1966) within Black communities reflect a culturally adaptive means of keeping people (especially men) away from the instruments of a repressive power structure.

While measures should be taken to safeguard all people who might be subjected to unethical, insensitive, and abusive practices in some court systems and by some police officers, we should emphasize that NBAC is supportive of programs that are designed to remove intoxicated drivers from the nation's highways. To promote this effort we advocate for increased services that are sensitive to Black culture and give recognition to the historical experiences of Blacks in White America. The need to educate the Black community about how to use the court system and to become involved in activities that will lead to the prevention of drunk driving, is as important as the need to educate law enforcement and judicial personnel about the importance of understanding and improving relationships with Black people. Before convicting a person for drunk driving, the courts should determine that all of the benefits that accrue to the person by law have been made available to him or her. Such benefits should include an assessment to determine if the person is a problem drinker, regardless of the person's ability to pay. Persons or agencies making DWI assessments should demonstrate their ability to understand and relate to the person being assessed, so that valid and useful information can be obtained to guide the court in making appropriate decisions. Personnel must, therefore, be able to understand and respect the divergent values, beliefs and customs of Black DWI persons from cultural backgrounds different from their own. A person interfacing with the criminal justice system must be assessed not only on the basis of cultural specificity but on socio-economic background as well.

In 1983, NBAC established a "Black Alcoholism Institute" (BAI) in cooperation with Howard University's School of Social Work. The BAI brings together some of the leading Black authorities in the field of alcohol abuse and Black people to provide intensive training sessions twice a year. The BAI can provide training programs that are specifically designed for the wide array of judicial and police staff who are involved with DWI cases. Training can be obtained by staff who attend the scheduled Institutes that are held in Washington, D.C. in June, or special training package that can be developed and implemented on site.

At another level NBAC will be working with the Black media associations to sensitize them to the influence of advertising and drinking. The goal is to have radio announcers who target the youth market with soulful music, and Black talk show hosts to take the lead in discussing the problem of alcohol-related accidents among Black people. They will also work with NBAC in identifying entertainers who will volunteer to make culturally-specific public service announcements. Entertainers and Black leaders will be used on posters and their messages conveyed in pamphlets and newspaper articles.

NBAC will work with state representatives to encourage legislation for a 21 minimum purchase and drinking age law. In a 1984 survey conducted by NBAC to determine the views of members and associates on the recommended age for persons to purchase and drink alcohol, the overwhelming majority of the respondents were in favor of 21 as the minimum for one to purchase and drink alcohol. Some 90 percent of the respondents recommended that alcohol education be integrated into the school curriculum as early as kindergarten. A significant number of respondents recommended stiffer penalties for persons with more than one DWI offense.

The thrust of the BADD campaign is at the community level and is implemented primarily by NBAC State Chapters and members through *Community Education Networking Conferences*. These conferences are designed to stimulate dialogue for the purpose of (1) educating the community leaders and the community about the seriousness of drunk driving and how it and other alcohol-related problems impact on the Black community; (2) networking with other organizations, agencies and institutions to promote working relationships and to bridge the communication gap between agencies like the police and courts. The expected outcome from these efforts will be increased awareness about drunk driving, better cooperation between the community and agencies responsible for DWI services, more appropriate and effective services for DWI offenders, and the reduction of the incidence of drunk drivers.

The period when emphasis is placed on BADD activities is during the month of February, which is Black History month, and in December during the Christmas Holidays. NBAC members engaged in drunk driving awareness activities in Black communities are encouraged to (1) learn the community; (2) determine who the key actors are; (3) involve the key actors in planning community education forums; (4) allow the community a chance to talk about their previous experiences with law enforcers to clear the air, before seeking their participation in the drunk driving campaign; and (5) seek volunteers from the community who can be trained to serve as public speakers.

CONCLUSION

It is extremely important for anyone working with the Black community around issues that relate to the involvement of increased police and criminal court involvement that could result in the arrest and imprisonment of other Blacks, to first understand the cultural dynamics that are involved. There is a need for both the Black community and law enforcement personnel to work toward bridging the communication gap to increase the effectiveness of any program that is designed to reduce the incidence of drinking drivers who fail to consider the damage they can cause to innocent victims.

The Black community must come to grips with the fact that alcohol is involved in far too many deaths, injuries, and illnesses, and be prepared to join forces with others to educate young people to prevent them from anesthetizing their minds and bodies to escape to what they might think is a better life. It is necessary that a coming together of "Black institutions, community leaders, and professionals (to) become aware of the impact of alcohol use/abuse on Black males (in particular and all Blacks in general), and consequently take action to minimize alcohol-related fatalities, illnesses, accidents, social problems, and mental health problems that currently harm and destroy the Black community" (Harper, 1981).

REFERENCES

Fell, J.C. Alcohol Involvement in Traffic Accidents: Recent Estimates From the National Center for Statistics and Analysis. NHSTA technical report No. DOT-HS-806269, Springfield, Virginia.

Gary, L.E. *Black Men.* Beverly Hills: Sage Publications, 1981.

Harper, F.D. *Alcohol Abuse and Black American.* Alexandria: Douglass Publishers, Inc., 1976.

Harper, F.D. Alcohol use and abuse. In *Black Men.* Beverly Hills: Sage Publications, 1981. p. 169–179.

Harvey, W.B. Alcohol abuse and the Black Community: A contemporary analysis. *Journal of Drug Issues, Inc.* Winter 1985 pp. 82–91.

Hyman, M. et al. Ascertaining police bias in arrest for drunken drivers. *Quarterly Journal of Studies on Alcohol.* 1972, 33, 148–159.

Hodges, H. et al. Race and the treatment of alcoholism in a southern state. In Alcohol abuse in the Black community: A contemporary analysis, *Journal of Drug Issues, Inc.* Winter 1985 p. 82.

Larkins, J.R. Alcohol and the Negro: Explosive issues. Zebulon, North Carolina: Record Publishing Company, 1965.

National Institute on Alcohol Abuse and Alcoholism. *Alcohol Health and Research World.* Washington: U.S. Government Printing 7:(1), 1982.

United States Department of Transportation, National Highway Traffic Safety Administration. *Alcohol and highway safety 1984: A Review of the State of the Knowledge.* Washington: US Government Printing Office, 1985.

United States Department of Transportation, National Highway Traffic Safety Administration. *The Use of Safety Checkpoints for DWI Enforcement.* Springfield, Virginia: National Technical Information Service, 1983.

Zax, M., et al. A Survey of Prevalence of Alcoholism in Monroe County, New York, 1961. In Harper *Alcohol Abuse and Black America.* Alexandria: Douglass Publishers, 1976, p. 40.

Driving Under the Influence
of Gender Discrimination

Brenda L. Underhill, M.S., C.A.C.

ABSTRACT. This paper argues that the problem of women and drinking and driving must be approached from two perspectives: (1) The design and implementation of DUI programs responsive to the particular needs of women and (2) A coordinated outreach effort to law enforcement agencies and the court system to increase the apprehension and referral of female offenders to drinking and driving programs. Statistics are examined which demonstrate that women are not being arrested, or convicted, or referred for drinking and driving in numbers at all equal to their participation in the problem. This paper further argues that coed drinking and driving programs where women are in the minority can epitomize the problems which alcoholic women encounter when seeking treatment in traditional programs which simply admit women for services without orienting those services to the specific needs of women.

The experiences of women in relation to drinking and driving exemplifies the difficulties encountered by women problem drinkers both in society and in traditional alcoholism treatment programs. Often, the woman's alcoholism/alcohol abuse is either ignored or protected (denied and enabled). When the problem is correctly identified as being alcohol-related, there is a punitive attitude toward her. This is demonstrated by society's stigma around women drinking and a gender-based double standard practiced by the alcoholism service delivery system. When a woman finally does seek help there is a lack of services which are oriented to meet her specific needs. In terms of women and DUI the following issues are observed: (1) Women are not being proportionately arrested, convicted or diverted for drinking and driving as compared to their

Brenda L. Underhill is the Executive Director of the Alcoholism Center for Women, 1147 South Alvarado Street, Los Angeles, California 90006.

Presentation at the National Council of Alcoholism, 1984, Annual Alcoholism Forum, April 14, 1984, Detroit, Michigan.

115

probable offense rate or in relation to men's rates and (2) When women are arrested, convicted and diverted to a DUI program, they are greatly outnumbered by male participants. This paper documents these two observations and discusses solutions.

The major difficulty in examining any issue related to women and alcohol problems is the lack of research available. This is particularly true of women and DUI. Thus, a definitive, empirically documented examination of the problem of women and DUI is not available. The statistics gathered here and my conclusions based on the correlation of these data is a start. Research and information of the problems encountered by women experiencing difficulties with alcohol other than DUI is examined in order to make some suggestions as to what the problems may be for women drinking drivers and what questions need to be addressed through further research. Evidence in service areas other than DUI that women actually experience barriers and opposition to entering treatment will be reviewed.

Thus this paper will examine the issue of drinking and driving in women in the larger context of women and alcoholism/alcohol abuse. The necessity for a twofold approach in working with women and DUI is outlined. This approach involves firstly the training of law enforcement personnel and the court system in the importance of arrest, conviction, and diversion for female drinking drivers and secondly, the design and implementation of DUI programs which are accessible and relevant to women.

SCOPE OF THE PROBLEM

It is relatively recent that the alcoholism profession and society in general have acknowledged that indeed, alcohol is an equal opportunity destroyer. Women are as susceptible to alcohol problems as their male counterparts. As Wilsnack (1982) points out, until very recently, most studies conducted their research almost exclusively on men, sometimes assuming the results applied equally to women. In part due to the women's movement of the 1970s, women and researchers began to challenge the assumption that alcoholism and alcohol abuse were primarily a male problem.

The number of women with alcohol problems was once assumed to be a minority. As Sandmaier (1980) points out, however, women's alcohol problems have been underestimated. Male bias in information collection methods utilized, such as the indicators which are more descriptive of male alcohol problems (e.g., public arrests) and the use of surveys based on consumption rates which are not adjusted to account for the biological differences between men and women, are some of the examples cited as contributing to the underestimation of women problem drinkers. Beckman's recent research (1981) into the influence of structural characteristics on women's utilization of alcoholism treatment services lends additional information on where women are seeking help for alcohol problems. She states that

> finally, the finding that only 15% of clients at alcohol-only facilities are women, plus the much higher reported percentages of women clients with alcohol-related problems in combined alcohol and drug programs (36%), women's crisis intervention programs (31%), and therapy with private practitioners (39%) support the contention that the majority of women alcohol abusers are not treated by mainstream alcoholism programs and women may prefer to utilize other types of programs.

This may not be a matter of preference on the part of women but rather a deficiency on the part of programs.

The California Women's Commission on Alcoholism (1983) presently estimates that between 35–50% of the alcoholic population are women, yet statewide make up less than 19% of those in treatment. This estimate is substantiated by the fact that more than 1 in 3 of those joining AA between 1977 and 1980 were women.

Examining available statistics in the area of drinking and driving reveals a similar pattern of underrepresentation and underutilization by women. Various studies have estimated women to comprise only 5–10% of those arrested (Hyman, 1968; Perrine, 1974; Argeriou and McCarty, 1982). Statistics in Los Angeles County indicate that only 10,440 of 105,922 or 9.9% of those arrested for drinking and driving in L.A. County in 1982 were women. The number of individuals referred to first offender DUI programs in 1982 in L.A. County are similar with only 2,945 of 23,096 or 12.8% of those referred being women. As McCormick (1983) cautions however, these statistics may be an underrepresentation of women who drink and drive.

> The hesitancy of the police to arrest women, and the leniency of the criminal justice system towards women have been cited

as factors which contribute to the underrepresentation of
women (Argeriou & Paulino, 1976; Seitz, 1978). Therefore it
is likely that women may significantly contribute to the growing
problem of alcohol related automobile accidents. (p. 2)

The hypothesis that women are not being arrested for DUI in
proportion to their involvement in the problem is extremely difficult
to document at this point through the existing research. A search of
the literature using the *Journal of Alcohol Studies* from 1976–1983
cited only two references in this eight year period to the subject of
women and drinking and driving. The Shaffer et al. study (1977)
investigated the social adjustment profiles of female drivers involved in fatal and nonfatal accidents and found a lack of deviancy
from the normative population in any undesirable pathological
sense. Of particular interest is a study done by Argeriou & Paulino
(1976) on the social characteristics and circumstances of arrest of 73
women arrested for driving while intoxicated and referred to a DUI
program in Boston. The results indicated that drinking and driving
was a necessary but not sufficient condition to account for the
arrests: 75% of the arrests were associated with a traffic accident,
violation, or the physical or verbal abuse of the arresting officer.
The authors conclude that

arrests of women for DUI usually occur only when accompanied by other factors which mandate arrest. Hence, the
unequal treatment of men and women by the police, while
apparently favorable to women in the short run, may well be
deleterious if it results in aiding problem drinking women to
keep their problems hidden. (p. 656)

STIGMA AND DOUBLE STANDARD

Obviously more research is needed to verify a more exact
incidence rate of women drinking drivers. The role of the social
stigma for women with alcohol problems and a societal double
standard in regards to the female driver, however, has been well
documented in the literature (Beckman, 1975; Blume, 1978; Curlee,
1967; Gomberg, 1974; Lawrence & Maxwell, 1962; Lindbeck,
1972; Marden & Kolodner, 1980; Rachal et al., 1975; Sterne &
Pitman, 1972; Sandmaier, 1978). It can be safely assumed this

information is pertinent to the problem of drinking and driving women. In addition to the problems created by external stigma for women drinkers is women's internalization of these factors. As Sandmaier (1980) states:

But the double standard on alcohol abuse does more than keep the problem drinker invisible. She is likely to internalize her culture's harsh judgement of her and learn to view herself with hopelessness and hatred. Studies repeatedly show that alcoholic women suffer more guilt, anxiety, and depression than alcoholic men, have lower self-esteem and attempt suicide more often. (p. 9)

In terms of women and DUI this greater stigma complicates an already complex situation. Not only does increased stigma result in increased denial but also in the isolation of the woman drinker. The solitary drinking pattern for women has also been documented by a number of researchers (Rathod & Thompson, 1971; Lisansky, 1957; Wanberg & Knapp, 1970). This pattern plus recent research that women actually encounter barriers and in fact experience opposition to entering treatment (Beckman & Amaro, 1982; Beckman & Kocel, 1981) underscores the importance of external intervention which DUI arrests provide.

When discussing services for women the most important issue to understand is that an effective women's program is *NOT* simply a previously all male facility which now admits women. Although it is true that certain characteristics of the disease of alcoholism apply equally to men and women, the recovery process involves learning to *live* with the disease. Since women's lives are very different from men's lives in our culture, it should be no surprise that women have different needs in recovery than men. Unless programs orient their services specifically to meet these needs, women will continue to be underrepresented in recovery programs. In California, women represent only 17% of participants in publicly funded programs. In Los Angeles County women represent only 19% of participants in programs funded with public money.

When the gap between the number of women with alcohol problems and the number of women seeking services was initially discovered, the "problem" was attributed to women. Women were assigned labels such as "more pathological" and "less motivated." A National Institute on Drug Abuse training program (1979) was designed to counter attitudes by counselors that alcoholic women were less motivated, and considered "more trouble" than their male counterparts in treatment.

In the mental health field Broverman (1970) studied the attitudes of men and women clinicians and found that they described a healthy female and a healthy male in very different terms. Specifically, a healthy woman was considered more submissive, less independent, less adventurous, less competitive, more excitable in minor crisis, more easily hurt, and more emotional than a mature healthy male. Therefore, the first issue which must be addressed is the attitudes of service providers. Specific training of staff in both sex role stereotypes and in the eroding effects of daily sex discrimination on self esteem is necessary to provide a recovery environment which enhances self-esteem and creates a healing environment for women.

In examining the issue of the design and delivery of services to women with alcohol problems, it is helpful to review some current research by Beckman (1982) on the barriers to treatment for alcoholic women. The following are some of the major findings from three of Beckman's studies: (1) Sources of referral for treatment are different for women than for men. Family and friends were found to be important sources of referral for ethnic women; (2) Women perceived more "costs" involved in entering treatment than men; (3) The number of referrals to treatment by the medical profession is low; (4) Alcoholic women are seeking services, but not necessarily in the alcohol program delivery system; (5) Women encountered more opposition to entering treatment from family and friends than males; (6) Women had fewer economic options than men; (7) Women expressed a desire for all women's groups; (8) A greater percentage of women clients were present in agencies that provided treatment for children and aftercare services and (9) Women were somewhat more likely to report problems with children as a consequence of excessive drinking while men somewhat more frequently reported job and legal consequences.

It is clear from examining this information on barriers along with current alcohol prevalence rates in women that women are not a "special" group with "special" needs. Women are rather, an *underserved* group with different needs. Some of these needs are as follows: (1) All women's groups where women can freely explore the connections between their recovery issues and their status as women; (2) Availability of child care—only a handful of residential programs across the United States allow for a woman to go into treatment with her children. Not only does this mean that she literally has to choose between her life and her children but also ignores the recovery needs of children who have been seriously affected by living in an alcoholic home; (3) Designing and implementing all services with an emphasis on increasing self-esteem for women. Specialized women's groups such as anger and assertion training where women can learn tools and techniques for expressing feelings and asserting needs on a daily basis, much of which is contrary to her socialization as a woman; (4) Outreach techniques which are geared to reaching women; (5) Facilities which are comfortable and safe. This includes parking lots that are well lit and facilities near public transportation; (6) Vocational training which retrains women in skilled positions (remembering that a woman makes 59 cents on the dollar to the man [NOW survey, 1980]). This is not a comprehensive list of women's needs in recovery. It is a sampling of some of what programs need to provide if they intend to truly serve women in any significant way.

In terms of barriers and services to women it is also critical that the diversity among and between women problem drinkers be recognized and accounted for by service providers. Beckman (1982) in her study on barriers and ethnic differences concludes '' . . . that barriers to treatment for ethnic women are more likely to stem from characteristics of the alcoholism service delivery system and its failure to meet the needs of ethnically diverse populations than from cultural values which dictate a negative predisposition to seeking alcoholism treatment'' (p. iv). Steps which Beckman feels need to be taken by providers to reduce these barriers include the following: (1) Provision of linguistically appropriate services; (2) Better trained staff in ethnic programs and the provision of education and training to ethnic women interested in the field of alcoholism and (3) implementation of treatment modalities which incorporate existing ethnic group cultural norms and support systems.

DUI PROGRAMS FOR WOMEN

It is proposed that in order to provide effective services DUI programs serving women need to take a twofold approach. This approach involves first, outreach and training to law enforcement and court personnel in the importance of the arrest, conviction, and referral of women drinking drivers. This training should include not only the basics of alcoholism and alcohol abuse specific to men but also the societal myths regarding women and alcohol much of which has been discussed in this paper. The critical role of the arresting officer in intervening in alcohol problems may best be approached through a training curriculum which focused on the "family syndrome" of alcoholism. In this way, the issue of the arresting officer's role as the protector of enabler when arrests of women are not made can be addressed in a nonthreatening manner by exploring similar roles in alcohol problem families. This training would have additional educational benefits to law enforcement personnel who regularly deal with domestic violence situations, the majority of which involve alcohol abuse.

The second part of this approach involves the design and implementation of DUI services which specifically address the problems of women drinkers. In this way the woman is encouraged to focus on her own behavior and responsibility as a driver. As with all alcohol-related counseling, individual and group sessions need to be supportive and directive in such a way that a woman can explore the aspects of her life which brought her into alcohol-related legal problems. These sessions are designed with an understanding of the considerable stigma borne by problem drinking women which figures so heavily against them seeking further help. She will be introduced to all female groups and to an atmosphere in which she can explore her problems with women of similar experience. Thus, she will not be the only person in the room facing gender based stigma, the complications to family life of her arrest, or the financial or safety burdens particular to women as is the case in most DUI programs. Part of the follow-up procedures should include appropriate referrals which take into account the unique needs of women in the areas of safety, employment, transportation, and child care as well as supportive environments in which to meet other women dealing with alcohol-related problems. The specific orientation of DUI services to the needs of women along with systematic outreach to law enforcement and court personnel is critical if women drinking drivers are to be seriously addressed.

IMPLICATIONS FOR RESEARCH

There is an obvious need for research in the area of women and drinking and driving. The exact incidence of women and drinking and driving is yet to be substantiated. The extent to which law enforcement personnel continue to ignore or protect the drinking and driving woman remains a "guesstimate" at best. To what extent the new stricter drinking and driving laws are effecting these rates also needs to be investigated.

Researching the experiences of women and DUI also offers the opportunity to gather important missing information on women and problem drinking in general. Such issues as to what extent an all women's environment enhances recovery, what effects an all women's approach has on the completion rates of women participants and the degree to which recidivism is reduced are some of the current questions without answers in the field of alcoholism today. The extensive record keeping system required by DUI programs easily lends itself to such evaluation. This research could be invaluable not only to women's services but also to increasing the effectiveness of alcohol services to all participants. Most important of all, increasing the effectiveness of DUI programs in general and decreasing the recidivism rate of drinking and driving women is crucial in efforts to reduce the enormous human and financial cost of drinking and driving.

CONCLUSIONS

Having examined the case of women and DUI, we are left with a striking comparison between specific issues of women drinking drivers and those faced by women problem drinkers in general. Firstly, the embarrassingly low arrest rate corresponds with the notion that women's alcohol problems are simply not taken seriously. By sending women home with a "warning," law enforcement officers are inadvertently reinforcing the myth that it's "no big deal." This allows women offenders to further deny that alcohol is interfering with their lives. Similarly, we continue to find women alcoholics—still drinking—sitting in the offices of physicians, psychiatrists and therapists being told that their problem is anything but alcoholism. This misdiagnosis in general is reflected by the low conviction rates for drinking and driving women. Thus, in the case of DUI, low arrests and conviction rates are mere manifestations of the commonly held beliefs that alcoholism is not a serious problem or not a primary problem. Once women "overcome" the disproportionate arrest rates, they are diverted. Similarly, once women break through social barriers and the prejudices of physicians and psychiatrists—those who must be convinced that alcohol is the problem—women are referred. But now it is important to look at what programs women are being diverted—referred. This is probably the most alarming similarity between the issues drinking and driving women and women problem drinkers face. DUI programs, like the overwhelming majority of recovery programs, are designed with men in mind. The same barriers are present in both kinds of programs such as the lack of child care, inaccessible sites, and prohibitive costs. The program curriculum of both range from being inappropriate or irrelevant at best to counterproductive and detrimental at worst. In short, programs either ignore women completely or perpetuate the stereotypes of women problem drinkers. Either way they fail to meet the needs of their women participants.

In both DUI programs and recovery programs, enrollment of women is much lower than their male counterparts. Statistically, men are more than twice as likely to be in treatment programs than women. This reflects the ongoing struggle of the alcoholism profession to provide parity of services.

Lastly, the DUI specialists and the recovery service providers, as well as alcoholism researchers continue to give little or no attention to women specifically. The failure to address women's specific needs, either in research or programatically, perpetuates the denial that women's problems with alcohol abuse exist and are as serious as men's problems.

REFERENCES

Argeriou, M. and McCarty, D. *Driving Under The Influence of Liquor in Massachusetts: A Study of Recidivism.* Report to Massachusetts Department of Public Health, Division of Alcoholism, Boston, MA, 1982.

Argeriou, M. and Paulino, D. "Women Arrested for Drunken Driving in Boston: Social Characteristics and Circumstances of Arrest." *Journal of Alcohol Studies*, 1976, 37, 5, 648–658.

Beckman, L. "Women Alcoholics: A Review of Social and Psychological Studies." *Journal of Studies of Alcohol.* 1975, 36:797–824.

Beckman, L. and Kocal, K. "Women's Utilization of Alcoholism Treatment Services: The Influence of Structural Characteristics. Study in preparation for publication, Women and Alcohol Project, Alcohol Research Center, UCLA, February, 1981.

Beckman, L. and Amaro, H. "Barriers To Treatment Among Anglo Women Alcoholics." Study in preparation for publication, Women and Alcohol Project, Alcohol Research Center, UCLA, 1982.

Beckman, L. and Amaro, H. "Barriers to Treatment Among Women Alcoholics: Ethnic

Brenda L. Underhill

Differences." Study in preparation for publication, Women and Alcohol Project, Alcohol Research Center, UCLA, 1982.

Blume, S. "Diagnosis, Casefinding and Treatment of Alcohol Problems in Women." *Alcohol Health and Research World*. 1978, 3 (Fall), 10–22.

Broverman, I. et al. "Sex-Role Stereotypes and Clinical Judgements of Mental Health." *Journal of Consulting and Clinical Psychology*, 1970, 34:1.

California Women's Commission on Alcoholism, *Definition of Women's Services*. Unpublished paper, 1983.

Curlee, J. "Alcoholic Women: Some Considerations For Further Research." *Bulletin of the Menninger Clinic*, 1967, 31, 154–163.

Gomberg, E.S. "Women and Alcoholism." *Women In Therapy: New Psychotherapies For A Changing Society*. V. Franks and V. Burtle, eds. New York. Brunner/Mazel, 1974.

Hyman, M. "The Social Characteristics of Persons Arrested for Driving While Intoxicated." *Quarterly Journal of Studies on Alcohol*, 1968, 4, 138–177.

Lawrence, J. and Maxwell, M. "Drinking and Socioeconomic Status," *Society, Culture, and Drinking Patterns*, ed. D.J. Pittman, and C.R. Snyder, New York; John Wiley and Sons, 1962.

Lindbeck, V. "The Woman Alcoholic: A Review of the Literature." *International Journal of the Addictions*, 1972, 7, 567–580.

Lisansky, E.S. "Alcoholism In Women: Social and Psychological Concomitants: Social History Data." *Quarterly Journal of Studies on Alcohol*, 1957, 18, 588–623.

Marden, P. and Kolodner, K. *Alcohol Abuse Among Women: Gender Differences and Their Implications for the Delivery of Services*. Rockville, MD: NIAAA, 1980.

McCormack, A. "Divorced/Separated Women: High Risk For Alcohol Related Automobile Accidents." Unpublished paper, 1983.

National Institute of Drug Abuse, *NIDA Training in Women Treatment, II*. Department of Health, Education, and Welfare, Washington, D.C., 1979.

Perrine, M. "Alcohol and Highway Safety," *Alcohol and Health: A Second Report to the U.S.*, NIAAA, (DHEW) Publ. No. 75-212, Washington, D.C.: U.S. Government Printing Office, 1974.

Rachal, J. et al., *A National Study of Adolescent Drinking Behavior, Attitudes, and Correlates*. Research Triangle Park, North Carolina, Research Triangle Institute, 1975.

Rathod, H. and Thompson, I.G. "Women Alcoholics: A Clinical Study." *Quarterly Journal of Studies on Alcohol*, 1971, 32:45–52.

Sandmaier, M. *Alcohol Programs For Women: Issues, Strategies and Resources*. Rockville, MD: National Clearinghouse for Alcohol Information, NIAAA, 1978.

Sandmaier, M. *The Invisible Alcoholics*. New York; McGraw Hill, 1980.

Seitz, L. "The Woman Alcoholic: A Hidden Problem." *Journal of the Tennessee Medical Association*, 1978, 71, 4, 295–296.

Shaffer, J. et al. "Social Adjustment Profiles of Female Drivers Involved in Fatal and Nonfatal Accidents." *American Journal of Psychiatry*. 1977, 134, 801–804.

Sterne, M. and Pittman, D. *Drinking Patterns in the Ghetto*, V.2, St. Louis, MO: Social Science Institute, Washington University, 1972.

Wanberg, K. and Knapp, J. "Differences in Drinking Symptoms and Behavior of Men and Women Alcoholics." *British Journal of Addictions*, 1970, 64

Wilsnak, S. "Alcohol Abuse and Alcoholism in Women." *Encyclopedia Handbook of Alcoholism*, ed. E.M. Pattison and E. Kaufman, New York: Gardner Press, 1982.

Characteristics of Men and Women Arrested for Driving Under the Influence of Liquor

Milton Argeriou, Ph.D.
Dennis McCarty, Ph.D.
Deborah Potter, M.A.
Linda Holt, B.A.

ABSTRACT. Comparisons of three populations of male and female DUIL offenders were carried out on a variety of descriptive measures. Repeat offenders differ from first offenders on all measures regardless of sex. Repeat offender males and females resemble each other closely as do first offender males and females. Compared to their first offender counterparts, repeat offender males and females drink more often, get drunk more often, abuse drugs in proportionately greater numbers, utilize more alcohol treatment services, have fewer economic resources, and exhibit greater impairment as a result of their drinking. The observed increase in DUIL arrests of females and their similarity to males in terms of problem drinking and drinking problems requires that intervention strategies be sensitive to the needs of both sexes.

The description of the typical drinking driver published in the U.S. Department of Transportation's landmark report on Alcohol and Traffic Safety (U.S. Department of Transportation, 1968) was based on ten studies which comprised the core of the alcohol and traffic safety literature at that time. Since that report, the volume of information describing the drinking driver has increased dramatically. For example, a review of the literature on the characteristics of individuals arrested and convicted of driving while intoxicated

Milton Argeriou, Dennis McCarty, and Deborah Potter are the research principals of Alcohol and Health Research Services, Inc., Stoneham, MA 02180.

Linda Holt is on the staff of the Research Division of the Department of Correction, Commonwealth of Massachusetts, Boston, MA 02111.

Address comments to: Milton Argeriou, Executive Director, Alcohol and Health Research Services, Inc., 134 Main Street, Stoneham, MA 02180.

127

conducted approximately ten years later examined 650 separate reports (Moskowitz et al., 1979).

Descriptions of drinking drivers usually address one or more of the following categories of variables: demographics, driving behavior, drinking practices, or personality and stress variables (U.S. Department of Transportation, 1978). A basic objective of these studies is to expand existing knowledge about drinking drivers in order to deal more effectively with these individuals and the problem of drinking and driving.

Unfortunately, few studies have provided information about women, even though they comprise approximately 13%[1] of those arrested for driving under the influence of liquor. Moreover, this lack of research attention exists despite evidence that women arrested for drinking and driving exhibit high levels of social pathology (Argeriou and Paulino, 1976; Argeriou et al., in press) and that the proportion of women arrested is increasing.[2]

A similar deficiency in the alcohol treatment evaluation literature has been noted by Vannicelli (1984), who sees sexist bias among investigators as being a significant factor contributing to the deficiency. While the lack of data on women in the alcohol and traffic safety literature parallels the deficiencies found by Vannicelli (1984), it appears that the lack of attention to drinking driving women is due more to the difficulty of obtaining a sample of women large enough to conduct meaningful analyses than to sex bias. As indicated by Perrine (1975) drinking and driving problems are a predominantly male domain, " . . . males comprise a larger proportion of: licensed drivers (about two-thirds), drivers sampled during roadside surveys (about 80%), fatally injured drivers (about 90%), as well as virtually all convicted DWIs (about 98%)."[3] Given this, it is clear that access to a data base containing sufficient numbers of men and women drinking drivers represents a rare opportunity to increase the level of knowledge and understanding in this area. The data base we examined was the Massachusetts Division of Alcoholism Management Information System (McCarty and Argeriou, 1983). In addition, data were abstracted from files maintained by the Massachusetts Department of Correction.

BACKGROUND

On September 1, 1982, the Massachusetts General Court enacted legislation modifying the penalties and court practices relative to the offense of Driving Under the Influence of Liquor (DUIL), Chapter

373 of the Acts of 1982. The new law increased fines imposed for drunk driving, established mandatory license suspension, and made sharp distinctions in the manner in which repeat offenders would be managed by the court. Specifically, second offenders are assessed a minimum fine of $300, lose their license for two years, and are incarcerated for a minimum of seven days. In lieu of incarceration, offenders may participate in a 14-day residential alcohol treatment program as a condition of probation. Third offenders are fined a minimum of $500, lose their license for five years, and must serve a term of imprisonment not less than 60 days nor more than two years.

Court management of first offenders under Chapter 373 is essentially the same as it was under previous legislation. Cases are usually continued without a finding and offenders are assigned to participate in an eight week driver education program as a condition of probation. However, a minimum 30 day license suspension is now mandatory for first offenders. Incarceration and a one year license loss is also possible but seldom imposed. The establishment of specific minimum mandatory sentencing alternatives according to frequency of prior DUIL offenses has effectively caused the courts to function as screening mechanisms which sort offenders into first, second, and multiple offender subgroups. Because each subgroup participates in separate punishment rehabilitation programs, access to the records of these programs provides the opportunity to describe and compare these "naturally" occurring subgroups.

The present report examines these groups of DUIL offenders: first offenders assigned to one of the twenty-eight Driver Alcohol Education Programs, second offenders assigned to the Rutland 14-day residential program, and offenders assigned to state and county correctional facilities. Sex differences within and among offender subgroups are given particular attention throughout the analyses and provide the major focus of this report.

METHOD

Sources and Nature of Data

DUIL offenders assigned to any of the twenty-eight first offender Driver Alcohol Education Programs (DAE) or the second offender 14-day residential program at Rutland State Hospital are entered into the Division of Alcoholism Management Information System (MIS) (McCarty & Argeriou, 1983). MIS files contain three types of client data. The admission interview is completed at intake and records the patient's age, sex, race, marital status, education, employment status, and resources for paying health care. In addition, the admission date and the source of referral are recorded. If the admission interview is not completed correctly, the client is not added to the MIS data base and the program cannot be credited for his/her treatment. The second source of patient information is the client profile. The profile assesses client functioning and living arrangements at admission, obtains a brief history of alcoholism treatment during the past year, and requests data on drinking patterns and the amounts drunk. Counselors complete the profile by rating the client's alcohol involvement and health, work, and social impairment. A discharge form is completed at termination of client participation. Reason for discharge is noted along with measures of drinking, socio-economic functioning, and counselor ratings of improvement. In fiscal 1984 (July 1, 1983 through June 30, 1984), 18,982 individuals were admitted to the DAE programs and 2,412 admissions to the Rutland Program were reported.

Some DUIL second offenders and all multiple DUIL offenders found guilty are incarcerated for varying periods of time in state and county correctional facilities. In calendar year 1983, 2,440 individuals were committed to 15 county jails and houses of correction. Age, sex, marital status, education, type and length of sentence to be served, committing court, and county of commitment are recorded on admission and release sheets maintained by the Department of Correction. Although these data are less extensive than the MIS information collected by the Division of Alcoholism they are sufficient to provide a basic description of the incarcerated population of DUIL offenders and allow comparisons among offender subgroups.

RESULTS

Subgroup Characteristics

The proportion of women in each subgroup of DUIL offenders decreases as the severity of sentence associated with that subgroup increases. Women comprise 13% of the DAE participants, 9% of the Rutland participants, and 3% of those incarcerated. Women in correctional facilities and in the Rutland program are similar in age

(M = 32.0). They are older than the DAE women (M = 30.3) and all male offenders, regardless of subgroup. There is essentially no difference in mean age among males in DAE (M = 30.5), Rutland (M = 30.6), or jail (M = 30.1).

Incarcerated women exhibit the highest proportion of divorce/ separation (41%) followed by women at Rutland (38%) and DAE women (32%). The proportions of divorce/separation among the subgroups of men are similar (17–22%) and significantly lower than the proportions exhibited by the women. Other analyses show rates of divorce/separation increase with age, regardless of sex or subgroup. However, when age is held constant, women offenders within subgroups continue to exhibit higher rates of divorce/ separation than their male counterparts. This would seem to indicate that risk of DUIL arrest among divorced/separated women is higher than other groups of men and women.

Comparisons of mean educational levels show little difference between men and women within offender subgroups. Across subgroups, educational level decreases in a parallel manner for males and females as one moves from DAE participants to Rutland participants to those incarcerated. (See Table 1.)

The racial composition of DUIL offenders was available for the DAE and Rutland programs only. The proportions of non-whites in these subgroups (i.e., 3–6%) are similar to the proportionate representation of non-whites (6.2%) in the general population of Massachusetts (U.S. Department of Commerce, 1983).

A comparison of the types of sentences received by men and women show proportionately more women than men receiving weekend sentences. The difference may be related to the fact that weekend sentences are more often given to 2nd offenders than to multiple offenders and that women are less likely than men to be multiple offenders (Argeriou and McCarty, 1982).

Additional Characteristics of DAE and Rutland Males and Females: Socio-Economic Indicators

Unemployment among men and women at Rutland is highly similar (11%) and highly dissimilar from their counterparts in the DAE program (5%). The same is true for the comparative proportions of Rutland men and women exhibiting no health insurance coverage (42%) and their DAE counterparts (27%). The comparative lack of socio-economic resources among Rutland participants

DRUNK DRIVING IN AMERICA

Table 1

Characteristics of DUIL Offender Subgroups by Sex (in percent)

Characteristic Level	DAE		Rutland		Incarcerated	
	Males (N=16,568)	Female (N=2,413)	Males (N=2,185)	Females (N=227)	Males (N=2,364)	Females (N=76)
Age						
Thru 19	10.0	8.7	3.6	2.2	4.2	5.3
20-24	28.2	28.1	30.4	26.0	29.8	17.1
25-34	33.4	34.8	39.8	36.1	40.8	40.8
35-44	15.8	17.0	15.2	20.7	15.9	26.3
45-54	7.7	8.0	6.6	11.9	7.0	9.2
55+	4.9	3.4	4.4	3.1	2.3	1.3
Mean	30.5	30.3	30.6	32.2	30.1	32.0
SD	11.2	10.4	10.2	10.1	9.4	9.3
Marital Status						
Single	56.3	51.6	58.0	48.9	57.8	42.1
Married	26.5	16.0	19.6	13.2	23.8	17.1
No longer married	17.3	32.4	22.4	37.9	18.4	40.8
Education					*	*
8 or less	5.0	2.2	6.6	4.0	7.9	2.0
9-11	17.4	15.1	22.2	20.7	29.2	27.5
12	43.9	44.4	46.0	45.8	47.8	39.2
13+	33.7	38.3	25.2	29.5	15.1	31.4
Mean	12.5	12.7	12.0	12.1	11.3	11.9
SD	4.5	3.7	3.9	2.0	2.0	1.9
Race						
White	94.3	97.8	95.7	96.0	**	**
Black	2.7	1.1	1.3	1.3		
Hispanic	2.4	.7	2.7	.9		
Other	.7	.4	.4	1.8		
Sentence Type						
Weekend					18.0	25.0
Non-Weekend					82.0	75.0

* Numbers of males and females reduced to 2,356 and 51, respectively.
** Data were not available for incarcerated offenders.

and among women, in particular, is clearly shown in the proportions of program participants receiving public assistance. One-fourth (27%) of the Rutland women and 15% of the Rutland men receive public assistance. In contrast, 14% of the DAE women and 7% of the DAE men receive assistance. These differences are reflected in the subgroup comparison of annual income.

Legal Involvement

Over twice as many Rutland men and women as DAE participants have been taken into protective custody in the past year. Moreover, the absolute proportions of protective custody arrests among Rutland men (18%) and women (14%) are of interest. They show almost one of every five Rutland men and over one of every ten Rutland women were sufficiently intoxicated in a public place as to warrant police intervention to ensure their safety. Other alcohol-related arrests among all subgroups are of lesser magnitude but continue to exhibit the same relative differences in proportion.

Alcohol Treatment Past Year

The involvement of Rutland men and women in previous alcohol treatment is essentially identical in proportion (30%) and significantly greater than the comparative proportions of DAE men and women (7% and 8%, respectively). It is likely that the observed difference in previous alcoholism treatment involvement between Rutland and DAE participants is related to the greater involvement of second offenders in the alcoholism treatment community resulting from their first and/or second DUIL arrest.

Alcohol and Drug Involvement

Rutland participants generally drink more and get drunk more often than DAE participants. Rutland women exhibit a higher average BAC (.179%) than Rutland men (.166%), and this relative difference is also observed among DAE women (.166%) and men (.158%). This finding may be related to similar drinking patterns and differing body weights, or it may reflect police practice of arresting women only if they are highly intoxicated (Argeriou and Paulino, 1976).

The proportions of drug abuse among Rutland men and women are similar (18%) and three times the proportions of drug abuse among DAE men and women (6%).

Counselor Ratings and Recommendations

Based on ratings by counselors, Rutland men and women again resemble each other more than they resemble their counterparts in the DAE program. As before, the relative differences between

programs reflect increased problem severity among Rutland participants in comparison to DAE participants. These differences in
perceived severity of impairment are mirrored in the differences
between programs in the proportions of participants who are
recommended for further treatment. More than ninety percent of
Rutland men and women, respectively, are recommended for
further treatment. Less than half of the DAE participants receive this
recommendation. Recommendations to Alcoholics Anonymous are
also more likely among Rutland participants (82%) than among
DAE participants (25%).

In summary, the data provided in Table 2 show greater similarity
between men and women within the DAE and Rutland Programs,
respectively, than across programs. The data also show greater
deteriorioation and decreasing resources among Rutland participants
than among DAE participants. Compared to their DAE counterparts, Rutland men and women drink more, get arrested more often,
utilize alcohol treatment services more often, have fewer economic
resources, and exhibit more impairment as a result of their drinking
behavior. As a consequence, the need for continued treatment
among the Rutland participants is higher than among those attending
the DAE program.

DISCUSSION

The data examined here present a clear picture of the differences
between first and repeat DUIL offenders. In every instance, the
difference is substantively, if not statistically significant. Repeat
offenders represent a select group of individuals who exhibit a variety
of problems related to or associated with their abuse of alcohoi.

The lack of difference between males and females within the
offender subgroups was unexpected. Women differed little from the
men with respect to the problems and need for treatment they
exhibited. In some respects, DUIL women may need greater
assistance because they lack some of the social supports available
to the men observed in this study. For example, women were more
often divorced/separated and more socio-economically deprived.

The relatively high proportion of drug abuse among DUIL second
offenders makes it clear that caregivers must be capable of dealing
with dual addictions. Focus upon alcohol abuse to the exclusion of
other addictive substances is likely doomed to failure.

Table 2

Behavioral Characteristics of DUIL Offenders Admitted

to the DAE and Rutland Programs by Sex (in percent)

Characteristic	Driver Alcohol Education		Rutland	
	Males (N=16,568)	Females (N=2,413)	Males (N=2,195)	Females (N=227)
Economic Indicators				
Unemployed	4.8	6.3	11.4	11.7
Public assistance	6.7	14.4	14.7	26.8
Annual income				
less than $1,000	5.1	8.1	10.7	17.3
more than $20,000	24.4	8.9	15.8	4.1
No health insurance	27.2	27.5	41.9	42.3
Legal Involvement past year				
Protective custody	7.5	5.0	19.3	13.7
Alcohol-related arrests	5.0	2.1	8.4	3.5
Alcohol Treatment Past Year				
Outpatient	1.8	2.5	12.3	17.2
Detoxification	2.1	3.0	5.6	6.6
Alcoholics Anonymous	4.3	6.6	23.3	23.8
No treatment	93.3	91.6	69.7	70.5
Alcohol and Drug Involvement				
Mean drinks per occasion	4.4	3.8	6.3	5.3
Mean drinking days per month	8.9	6.9	10.6	8.5
Mean most drinks	7.6	5.9	11.2	8.2
Mean days drunk past month	1.5	1.3	3.1	2.1
Mean drinks past month	49.4	36.3	92.4	60.1
Mean BAC at arrest [a]	.158	.166	.166	.179
Abusing drugs	6.3	6.1	13.2	17.7
Moderate/severe impairment	30.0	27.5	46.3	41.0
Counselor Recommendations				
Recommend more treatment	44.3	41.0	95.2	94.1
AA recommended	24.9	25.2	83.3	80.8

Note. Rutland and DAE clients differ significantly ($p < .01$) on all variables.

[a] excludes clients who refused to take the breath test or could not recall the reading.

Women constitute a relatively small proportion of the total population of those arrested for DUIL. However, this proportion has increased rapidly in recent years. Moreover, the data examined in this report show women parallel men in terms of alcohol-related behaviors, problems, and the need for treatment. Failure to consider women in efforts to differentiate DUIL offender subgroups and to devise treatment strategies appropriate to these subgroups is not justified. As Vannicelli (1984) has indicated, greater sensitivity to bias is needed among researchers to insure an increase in knowledge about problem drinking women and effective treatment for them.

REFERENCE NOTES

1. The proportion of women arrested for driving under the influence of liquor in Massachusetts is currently 12.8 percent. Based on F.B.I. Uniform Crime Report data for 1983, women comprise 12.7% of all DUIL arrests nationally. It must also be noted that although the proportion of women arrested for DUIL is relatively small, the absolute number of individuals involved is sizable: 155,316 women were arrested nationally in 1983.

2. An increase in the proportion of women arrested for driving under the influence of liquor has been observed in Massachusetts. In the Fiscal Year beginning July 1, 1979, women comprised approximately 10.1% of those arrested for driving under the influence of liquor. This proportion increased to 12.8% for Fiscal Year 1984. The Massachusetts increase is strikingly similar to the increase observed nationally during essentially the same time period: 9.7% in calendar year 1979 and 12.7% in 1983. Among women, DUIL arrests increased 68% compared to 28% among men during this five year period. (U.S. Department of Justice, 1984). These increases appear related to the increased pressure upon police to arrest drinking drivers, whatever their sex. Continued increases in the proportion of women arrested are likely because the role of women in American Society continues to undergo change. The proportion of women drivers is expected to increase in the coming years (U.S. Department of Transportation, 1978), as well as the proportion of women who may drink and drive (Williams and Klerman, 1984).

3. The proportion of convicted female DWI offenders stated by Perrine (1975) appears low in view of current arrest data (see note #2). His commentary regarding the preponderance of males remains accurate, nevertheless.

REFERENCES

Argeriou, M. and Paulino, D. (1976). Women arrested for drunken driving in Boston. Social characteristics and circumstances of arrest. *Journal of Studies on Alcohol,* (1976), *37,* 643–658.

Argeriou, M. and McCarty, D. (1982). Driving Under the Influence of Liquor in Massachusetts: A Study of Recidivism, Stoneham, MA: Alcohol and Health Research Services, Inc.

Argeriou, M., McCarty, D., and Blacker, E. (In Press). Criminality among individuals arraigned for drinking and driving in Massachusetts. *Journal of Studies on Alcohol.*

McCarty, D. and Argeriou, M. (1983). Massachusetts Alcoholism Management Information System User's Manual. Stoneham, MA: Alcohol and Health Research Services, Inc.

Moskowitz, H., Walker, J., and Gomberg, C. (1979). A comparison of demographic and psychosocial characteristics of DWI drivers, control drivers, and alcoholics. Los Angeles: University of California, Alcohol Research Center.

Perrine, M.W. (1975). The Vermont driver profile: A psychometric approach to early

identification of potential high risk drinking drivers. In Israelstam, S. and Lambert, S. (Eds.) Alcohol, Drugs, and Traffic Safety. Toronto: Addiction Research Foundation.
U.S. Department of Commerce (1983). 1980 Census of Population. General Social and Economic Characteristics: Massachusetts. Washington, D.C., U.S. Government Printing Office.
U.S. Department of Justice (1984). Crime in the United States 1983. F.B.I. Uniform Crime Reports. Washington, D.C., U.S. Government Printing Office.
U.S. Department of Transportation (1968). Alcohol and Highway Safety. Report to the U.S. Congress. Washington, D.C., U.S. Government Printing Office.
U.S. Department of Transportation (1978). Alcohol and Highway Safety. A Review of the State of Knowledge: Summary Volume. Washington, D.C., U.S. Government Printing Office.
Vannicelli, M. (1984). Treatment outcome of alcoholic women: The state of the art in relation to sex, bias, and expectancy effects. In Wilsnack, S.C. and Beckman, L.J. (Eds.) Alcohol Problems in Women, New York: The Guilford Press, pp. 369–412.
Williams, C.N. and Klerman, L.V. (1984). Female alcohol abuse: Its effects on the family. In Wilsnack, S.C. and Beckman, L.J. (Eds.) Alcohol Problems in Women, New York: The Guilford Press, pp. 280–312.

An Education Program for Collaterals of DWI Offenders

Robert J. McGrath, M.A., C.A.C.

ABSTRACT. Engaging family and significant others in the treatment of alcoholism and problem drinking is increasingly recognized as an important element in successful intervention. This article presents a rationale for involving collaterals of DWI (Driving While Intoxicated) offenders in a specially designed education program associated with a DWI school. A model for such a program, including recruitment strategies, is outlined.

INTRODUCTION

Drinking drivers are responsible for a significant portion of driving-related accidents, fatalities, and injuries (Fine & Scoles, 1974; U.S. National Institute on Alcohol Abuse and Alcoholism, 1979; Zylman, 1974). To address this major traffic safety concern, federally funded programs were initated in the late 1960s to prevent recidivism among drinking drivers. Despite the fact that the number and variety of drinking driver countermeasure programs has increased markedly since that time, a concomitant increase in the effectiveness of these programs has yet to be realized. A review of the literature suggests that DWI re-education schools have been successful in increasing participants' knowledge about alcohol and driving and improving attitudes regarding safe driving practices (Malfetti, 1976). However, drinking driver re-education schools have failed to alter recidivism rates to any significant extent (National Highway Traffic Safety Administration, 1974; Nichols,

Robert J. McGrath is Alcohol Treatment Coordinator at The Counseling Service of Addison County, Inc., 89 Main Street, Middlebury, Vermont 05753. This study was funded in part by a Prevention Grant to the Counseling Service of Addison County, Inc. from the Alcohol and Drug Abuse Division of the Vermont Department of Social and Rehabilitative Services.

Weinstein, Ellingstad, & Strukman-Johnson, 1978; Popkin, Lacey, Li, Stewart, & Waller, 1983).

Strategies of DWI re-education programs have been aimed primarily at educating convicted drinking drivers about the influence of alcohol on driving skills, prodding them to examine their patterns of alcohol misuse, and, when appropriate, recommending or sometimes mandating alcohol treatment. DWI programs have neglected the family and social support networks of offenders as a focus of intervention. This is significant in the light of research evidence supporting the value of involving family members in the treatment of alcoholics.

This paper presents a rationale for involving the family and friends of DWI offenders in the rehabilitative process and outlines an appropriate educational program for these collaterals. While this particular program is yet to be validated empirically, it is believed that family and significant other involvement in DWI programs may improve the effectiveness of these programs, and can serve as an important intervention for the collaterals themselves.

THE DRINKING DRIVER

Estimates of the incidence of serious problem drinking or alcoholism among convicted drunk drivers range as high as 60 to 80 percent (Selzer, 1979; Yoder & Moore, 1973). For these individuals, drunk driving is not an isolated incident but only one symptom of a much more pervasive problem with alcohol. It is a problem that may effect their health and can impair their social, marital, family, and vocational adjustment. Drinking drivers are, therefore, an appropriate target for prevention efforts aimed at reducing the risks of the development of more serious drinking problems as well as DWI recidivism.

Considering the number of offenders involved in this major public health problem, the potential for the positive impact of prevention efforts is tremendous. Nationally, driving while intoxicated was the most frequent offense committed in 1982 (U.S. Bureau of the Census, 1983). In Vermont, between July 1, 1983 and June 30, 1984, 2,967 individuals completed the state's DWI re-education program; this number was only slightly less than the approximately 3,000 individuals who were enrolled in state subsidized outpatient, detoxification, residential, and halfway house alcohol treatment programs combined. Three year recidivism rates for convicted DWI offenders are commonly in the 18 to 20 percent range (e.g. Merrill, 1983; Weeber, 1981).

Although some DWI programs mandate alcohol treatment for DWI offenders who are assessed as alcoholic, many programs remain strictly educational in nature and have no power to coerce high risk drinkers into treatment. The rates of successful referral to treatment programs are, not surprisingly, dismally low. Therefore, large numbers of alcoholics are enrolled and sometimes identified in DWI schools but opportunities to engage them in ongoing treatment are often missed.

A significant portion of DWI offenders have "intact" social support systems. Independent samples from Vermont (Merrill, 1983) and Mississippi (Weber, 1981) found 58 percent of offenders to be currently married. A study conducted in Phoenix, Arizona (Sandler, Palmer, Holmen, & Wynkoop, 1975) surveyed a population of drinking drivers and identified 37 percent as high risk problem drinkers. They found that 53 percent of this high risk group were currently married and only 13 percent had never been married. Moskowitz, Walker, and Gomberg (1979) found that social support networks of DWI offenders are more stable than those of chronic alcoholics enrolled in treatment but less stable than those of the population in general.

ALCOHOL AND THE FAMILY

The impact of alcohol abuse on families is well documented. In alcoholic families, the separation and divorce rate is four to eight times that of the general population (McCrady, 1982). The percentage of marital violence in these families is reported to be as high as 50 percent (Gerson, 1978). Estimates of child abuse cases in alcoholic families range as high as 25 percent (Johnson & Morse, 1963) and child neglect was found among all the children of alcohol abusers surveyed by Black and Mayer (1980). It is also clear that children of alcoholics are at high risk to become alcoholics themselves (Cotton, 1979).

The interactive effect of alcohol abuse on family life has led most professionals in the field to think of alcoholism as a family illness (Bowen, 1974; Johnson, 1973; Wegscheider, 1981). Alcoholism within the family serves to both perpetuate and maintain a variety of

maladaptive functioning patterns by its members. Wegscheider
(Filmmakers, 1980) suggests that the incidence of psychosomatic
illness among spouses of alcoholics is significantly higher than
among the general population. Many writers and researchers
(Black, 1982; Wegscheider, 1981; Woitiz, 1983) are investigating
the long term emotional impact on children who grew up in
alcoholic families. Self help support groups for adult children of
alcoholics are currently mushrooming throughout the country.

SIGNIFICANT OTHERS AND ALCOHOL TREATMENT

There has been a long and consistent trend of involving families
and significant others in the treatment of alcoholics. Historically,
however, alcohol treatment focused solely on the alcoholic as an
individual. Alcoholics Anonymous, perhaps the most significant
development in the treatment of alcoholics, had its beginnings in
1935 and gained national recognition by 1941. The needs of family
members of alcoholics were recognized and then addressed by the
formation of Al-Anon in 1952. In 1957, a self-help program for
teenagers of alcoholics, Alateen, was founded. In the sphere of
professional alcohol treatment, it was not long ago that many
residential alcohol treatment centers attempted to isolate the alcoholic from family contact during treatment. However, most residential programs for alcoholics have developed active, comprehensive
family treatment components. In fact, many residential programs
for alcoholics require a residential component for the family
members as well. Today, almost all competent outpatient alcohol
treatment programs routinely involve family members in treatment
and address issues of family dynamics.

Family therapy was called the most noteworthy recent advance in
the treatment of alcoholism by Keller in the Second Special Report
to Congress on Alcohol and Health (U.S. National Institute on
Alcohol Abuse and Alcoholism, 1974). Kaufmann & Pattison
(1982) state that "Family therapy and other systems interventions
have slowly emerged over the past decade as essential to the
treatment of alcoholism." With regard to this relatively new
movement, educating the family about alcohol and alcoholism is
almost always part of the family involvement and almost always
helpful (Kaufmann & Pattison, 1982). Kellerman (1974) states the
case for family involvement succinctly.

First, helping the families will multiply the recovery rate of alcoholic persons. Second, and of far greater importance, the spouses and children of alcoholic persons desperately need help themselves, not primarily to become agents of recovery for the alcoholic person, but to free themselves from the enslavement of alcoholism and to become human beings in their own right.

He goes on to suggest that

the family needs more help than the alcoholic person for the disrupted need more help than the disruptor.

Despite the fact that family treatment and education are well respected and almost necessary elements in designing a comprehensive alcohol treatment program, engaging the family in treatment is often a difficult task. Denial seems to play as central a role in the cognitive process of family members and significant others as in that of the alcoholic him/herself.

Gorman and Rooney (1979) studied both the denial of wives of alcoholics and their delay in seeking treatment. They found that events such as alcohol related arrests were often the earliest concrete episodes indicating alcohol problems in the family and that these episodes occurred an average of 7 years prior to the wives seeking help. Kellerman (cited by Brozan, 1976) estimated that a wife, on average, denies her husband's drinking problem for between 6 and 8 years and then waits another 2 years to seek help. Jackson and Kogan (1963) also document the denial and delay of help-seeking behavior in wives of alcoholics.

One could hypothesize that significant others also deny problem with drinking and driving as well. Yoder (1975) observed that 75 percent of DWI convictions in a California sample could have been prevented if friends and relatives had dissuaded from driving the person who had been drinking. Forty percent would have been prevented if the host had provided alternative methods of transportation and his guests had used these altenatives. More study is needed to determine to what extent this apparent lack of intervention by collaterals is indeed a result of denial, as other factors such as lack of knowledge and fear of confronting the drinking driver might be significant.

As great as the impact of initial denial of significant others is to the alcoholic drinker, it is the significant others' later recognition of a problem that often plays a vital role in engaging and keeping the alcoholic in treatment. "Intervention" (Johnson, 1978; Wegscheider, 1981), a therapeutic strategy in which the drinker's alcoholic behavior is confronted in a "family" meeting, is entirely dependent on family and significant others collectively using their influence on the alcoholic. Strug and Hyman (1981) found that alcoholics who made contact with alcohol treatment agencies did so most often as a result of pressure from network members, especially confidants who discouraged their drinking. They suggest the importance of identifying significant others who can cooperate with rehabilitation personnel, and stress the need to identify alcoholics *before the alcoholic's social support networks disintegrate*. Gorman and Rooney (1979) found that one of the most important antecedents to wives seeking help regarding an alcoholic spouse was confrontation by other family and friends regarding the severity of drinking problems within the family. This appeared to be a more important motivating factor in seeking help than such events as the arrest of a spouse, family violence, poor health due to alcoholism, or job loss. The involvement of family members in treatment has been found by a number of researchers (Berger, 1981; Codogan, 1973; Janzen, 1977) to be positively related to an alcoholic's completion of treatment regardless of whether that treatment was in a detoxification, residential, or outpatient setting.

If family and significant others need treatment themselves, and if they can play an important role in the recovery of the alcoholic, the question then becomes how to engage these individuals in treatment. More pointedly, if, as some researchers assert (Gorman & Rooney, 1979; Kellerman, 1974), families seek help most frequently when the family system is about to deteriorate, how can intervention occur earlier in the course of the disease? Many clinicians have reported strategies for working with families already under stress for alcohol problems. The research and writings in the area of engaging alcoholics and families into treatment, however, have been generally quite scanty, and material on early intervention in the alcoholic family system is almost non-existent.

CRISIS THEORY

Crisis theory (Rapaport, 1965) offers a pragmatic solution to the problem of early intervention with an alcoholic family or other close-knit alcoholic social system. The offender's family and significant others often experience the DWI arrest as a crisis. The subsequent legal encounters, financial burdens, transportation adjustments, and public disclosure are among the events which sustain the crisis. The resolution of the crisis may result in either a return to the individual's and system's previous level of functioning, a deterioration in functioning, or progression to a higher level of mental health. A timely intervention during the DWI crisis, even if it were short-term in nature, can provide positive long-term effects. According to crisis theory, the healthy resolution of such a crisis seems to be dependent on the following conditions: (1) a new perception of the problem brought about by new information, (2) resolution of feelings through awareness and catharsis, (3) new help seeking and utilization behavior.

THE FAMILY PROGRAM

A successful method for engaging family and significant others of DWI offenders which utilized crisis theory has been reported by McGrath and Pandiani (in press). They offered $50 rebates to participants in DWI schools who brought one or more family members or significant others to an 8 hour family education program which ran concurrently with the DWI offender's DWI re-education school. As a result of this strategy, approximately 46 percent of DWI school participants brought collaterals to the family program. A later study by McGrath (1984) netted a 66 percent collateral participation rate using the same strategy. When no rebates were offered, DWI school participants did not recruit collaterals for the family program. McGrath and Pandiani (in press) also found that those collaterals who attended the family program were indeed "significant" in the lives of the DWI offender. Seventy-five percent of the collaterals who completed the family program either lived with or were related to a DWI school participant. DWI school participants who brought collaterals to the family program were found to be just as likely to have serious drinking problems as those who did not bring family members. Therefore, a good portion of the high risk group in the DWI school did bring family or friends to the program.

The remainder of this paper will address the philosophy, goals, structure, content, and feasibility of a family education component attached to a DWI school. The DWI school, Project CRASH, is the State of Vermont's four session, 10 hour, re-education school for convicted drinking drivers and is quite similar to DWI programs described elsewhere (Stewart and Malfetti, 1980). This material is based on the author's experience in conducting six family programs which were composed of almost 100 family members and significant others of drinking drivers.

The family program identified three major goals: (1) to provide information about alcohol and the disease of alcoholism, (2) to provide an opportunity for collaterals to examine how their or someone else's drinking has affected their life, and (3) to introduce collaterals to resources that are available to help persons concerned with either their own or someone else's alcohol problems. The three program goals flow from what was previously outlined as the three elements necessary for the healthy resolution of a crisis.

At the first of the four classes of the standard DWI school for convicted drinking drivers, the participants were provided with written and oral information about the family program. They were advised about the goals, content and structure of the program and were assured that participation or non-participation in the family program would neither jeopardize nor help them in completing the DWI school and the subsequent return of their license. DWI school participants were advised that if a family member or significant other (over the age of 18) whom they referred to the family program subsequently completed that program, the offenders would receive a financial rebate of $50 on the DWI school fee of $115.00.

The family program consisted of three 2 1/2 hour group sessions followed by a 1/2 hour personal interview. Each group session included a lecture, film, and a group discussion with a brief break following the film. The family program was conducted concurrently with the last three meetings of the DWI school but in a different portion of the building. The group discussions were composed of 8 to 10 family participants and one staff leader. All personal interviews were scheduled within three weeks of the last group session.

Session 1: Alcohol and Alcoholism

The purposes of the first family session were to familiarize the participants with both the DWI school and family program objectives, to instill a basic understanding of the drug alcohol and how it relates to impaired driving, and to transmit knowledge about the disease of alcoholism. In order to reduce resistance of family program participants, they were told at the outset that approximately half of DWI offenders have serious drinking problems while the other half do not. Family program participants were also assured that they were not expected to police the drinking behavior of the DWI offenders. The family program was designed specifically to meet the needs of the family members and significant others. Although alcoholism can be looked at as a multidimensional rather than a unitary disorder, the program developers felt presenting information about alcoholism as a unitary progressive disease would be both pragmatic (Gitlow, 1980) and in concert with the treatment resources available to the family participants. The film "Chalk Talk on Alcohol—Revised" (Martin, 1974) was found to be a complement to the lecture material and stimulated a good deal of discussion. Typical and useful discussion questions and issues for the first group discussion included: What is alcoholism? What is problem drinking? Describe someone that you know who is alcoholic. Why do people drink? Is alcoholism hereditary? Is the alcoholic responsible for his/her behavior?

Session 2: Alcohol and the Family

This session focused on alcoholism as a family illness. Participants were given the opportunity to examine the impact of alcohol on their family by one of a variety of adapted self-report checklists. The concept of the "enabler" was addressed extensively and supported in the second session film, "Soft Is The Heart Of A Child," (Operation Cork, 1978) or a similar film that depicts the impact of alcoholism on the family and the role of the family in perpetuating the illness. Discussion focused on "enabling" and the paradox of "attempting to help someone with a drinking problem by not helping them."

Session 3: Help and Hope for Families

The goals of session 3 were to instill a sense of hope in members of the group who were suffering the consequences of problem drinking or alcoholism within the family, to outline coping skills for families, to describe treatment options and resources, and to have participants develop treatment or prevention plans for their famlies. Specific information about treatment resources, including local program names, places, and eligibility requirements, were outlined, and specific strategies for family members and friends addressing to the issue of alcoholism in the family were outlined. The movie "Intervention" (Johnson Institute, 1978) was shown. It dramatized a strategy through which family and friends confront an alcoholic and outlined a variety of the new behaviors that collaterals of alcoholics can begin to implement in order to alter maladaptive interactions with the alcoholic. Special suggestions proposed to the family program participants were collected from many excellent self-help books in this area (Johnson, 1973; Maxwell, 1976; Wegscheider, 1981).

Since many of the individuals in the family program were examining for the first time how alcoholism or problem drinking was affecting their family, the family program was often an emotional experience for them. Because the lecture and film portion of Session 3 elicited strong feelings from family group participants, it was imperative to facilitate a sensitive discussion of the relevant issues. In addition to assisting some people in making plans to confront a problem drinker, it was equally important to give permission to more hesitant collaterals to proceed at their own pace.

Individual Interview

The final individual interview was designed to help collaterals to summarize their learning, receive answers to any lingering questions, and develop a plan of continued treatment or prevention for themselves and the family. Since interviews of collaterals were scheduled just prior to that of the referring DWI school participants, it was possible for those collaterals to suggest to the interviewer possible topics to explore with the DWI school participants. It was made clear, however, that the collaterals could choose to have complete confidentiality throughout the family program. For collaterals and DWI school participants who agreed to it, program staff facilitated joint meetings to develop treatment plans or to pinpoint behaviors that will be warning signs for each of them in the future.

DISCUSSION

Persons who are convicted of drunk driving and who remain unrehabilitated represent a continued traffic safety threat both to themselves and to society. The large number of drunk drivers who are alcoholic and who also live in family situations represent a significant threat to the healthy functioning of their family systems and to each family member. The collaterals of these alcoholics are commonly in need of education or treatment services themselves and are often in an excellent position to positively influence the problem drinker.

Complementing an existing DWI re-education school for drinking drivers with a family education component during the crisis period can address the education and treatment referral needs of collaterals and may well enhance the effectiveness of the DWI school itself. In our experience, such programs have been well-received by family and friends of drinking drivers. In fact, staff conducting the family programs often have had to use strategies to limit inappropriate self disclosure among collaterals. Since the family program has been educational rather than therapeutic, group leaders have needed to maintain the appropriate boundaries as defined by the program goals and direct members who want or need treatment to the appropriate resource.

The most difficult aspect of implementing such a program is the recruitment of collaterals. As outlined previously (McGrath & Pandiani, in press) financial rebates have been an effective, albeit expensive, recruitment strategy. Programs may increase the fees in their DWI schools to offset the rebate and family program costs. Non-financial incentives to use collateral participation might also be explored. For example, DWI school participants who involved collaterals in a family program could have their licenses suspended for a shorter time than drinking drivers who did not bring collaterals to this course. Judges and probation officers who support the program might positively influence participation rates. Community knowledge and recognition of the program might well influence utilization rates significantly. It has been our experience that each successive family program has had a slightly higher percentage of collateral participation than the last. This may be explained, in part, by increasing public recognition and acceptance of the program as it has matured.

Clearly, drunk driving is a problem which is multidetermined. Determinants include factors such as public attitudes, alcohol availability, enforcement strategies, and rehabilitation efforts; these also are areas for intervention. The family program is potentially a valuable addition to the list of strategies currently being employed to combat drinking driving. It is our hope that others will be stimulated to engage family and significant others in DWI collateral programs.

A next step should be outcome research aimed at determining the impact of the family program on DWI recidivism rates, the DWI offender, collaterals, and the family system.

REFERENCES

Berger, A. Family involvement and alcoholic's completion of a multiphase treatment program. *Journal of Studies on Alcohol*, 1981, 30, 517–521.

Black, C. *It Will Never Happen to Me.* Denver: Mac Book, 1982.

Black, R. and Mayer, J. *An Investigation of the Relationship Between Substance Abuse and Child Abuse and Neglect.* National Center on Child Abuse and Neglect, Washington, DC: Department of Health, Education, and Welfare, Office of Human Development, 1980.

Bowen, M. Alcoholism as viewed through family systems theory and psychotherapy. *Annals of The New York Academy of Science* 1974, 233, 115–122.

Brozan, N. For every alcoholic, three or four others are direct victims who need help. *New York Times*, March 3, 1976, p. 39.

Codogan, D.A. Marital group therapy in the treatment of alcoholism. *Quarterly Journal of Studies on Alcohol, 1973, 34, 1187–1194.*

Cotton, N.S. The familial incidence of alcoholism: A review. *Journal of Studies on Alcohol*, 1979, 40, 89–116.

Filmmakers (Producer) and Filmmakers (Director). *The Family Trap* (Film). Minneapolis: Filmmakers, 1980.

Fine, E.W. and Scoles, P. Alcohol, alcoholism and highway safety. *Public Health Review*, 1974, 30, 423–436.

Gerson, L.W. Alcohol-related acts of violence: Who was drinking and where the acts occurred. *Journal of Studies on Alcohol*, 1978, 39, 1294–1296.

Gitlow, S.E. An overview. In S.E. Gitlow and H.S. Peyser (eds.), *Alcoholism: A Practical Treatment Guide.* New York: Grune & Stratton, 1980.

Gorman, J.M. and Rooney, J.F. Delay in seeking help and onset of crisis among Al-anon wives. *American Journal of Drug and Alcohol Abuse*, 1979, 6, 223–233.

Jackson, J. and Kogan, K. The search for solutions: Help-seeking patterns of active and inactive alcoholics, *Quarterly Journal of Studies on Alcohol*, 1963, 24, 449–472.

Janzen, C. Families in the treatment of alcoholism. *Journal of Studies on Alcohol*, 1977, 38, 114–130.

Johnson, B. and Morse, H. *The Battered Child: A Study of Children With Inflicted Injury.* Denver: Department of Welfare, 1968.

Johnson Institute (Producer), and Filmmakers (Director). *Intervention* (Film). Minneapolis: Filmmakers, 1978.

Johnson, V. *I'll Quit Tomorrow.* New York: Harper & Row, 1973.

Kaufman, E. and Pattison, E.M. Family and network therapy in alcoholism. In: E.M. Pattison and E. Kaufman (Eds.), *The Encyclopedic Handbook of Alcoholism.* New York: Gardner, 1982.

Kellermann, J.L. Focus on the family. *Alcohol Health and Research World*, 1974, Fall, 9–11.

Malfetti, J.L. Accountability for DWI programs. *Proceedings of the National DWI Conference*, Lake Buena, Florida, May 1976. Falls Church, Virginia: AAA Foundation for Traffic Safety, 1976.

Malfetti, J.L. and Winter, D.J. *Counseling Manual for Educational and Rehabilitative Programs for Persons Convicted of Driving While Intoxicated (DWI).* New York: Teachers College, Columbia University, 1980.

Martin, J. (Producer) and Abraham, M. (Director). *Chalk Talk on Alcohol—Revised* (Film). Aberdeen, Maryland: Kelly Productions, 1974.

Maxwell, R. *The Booze Battle*. New York: Praeger, 1976.

McCrady, B.S. Marital dysfunction: Alcoholism and marriage, in E.M. Pattison and E. Kaufman (Eds.), *The Encyclopedic Handbook of Alcoholism*. New York: Gardner, 1982.

McGrath, R.J. (collateral participation rates in a DWI school). Unpublished raw data, 1984.

McGrath, R.J. and Pandiani, J.A. Amount of financial rebate and collateral participation in a DWI school. *Journal of Alcohol and Drug Education*, in press.

Merrill, D.G. Education and therapy programs for drunk drivers: They work! *Proceedings of the DWI Colloquium*, San Diego, California, August, 1983. Falls Church, Virginia: AAA Foundation for Traffic Safety, 1983.

Moskowitz, H., Walker, J., and Gomberg, C. A comparison of demographic and psychosocial characteristics of DWI drivers, control drivers, and alcoholics. UCLA Alcohol Research Center of the Neuropsychiatric Institute, June 1979.

National Highway Traffic Safety Administration. *Alcohol Safety Action Projects: Evaluation of Operations—1974. Vol. II. Detailed analysis. Chapter 5. Evaluation of the Rehabilitation Countermeasure Activities.* (Report No. DOT/HS-801-729). Washington, D.C., 1974.

Nichols, J.L., Weinstein, E.B., Ellingstad, V.S., and Struckman-Johnson, D.L. The specific deterrent effect of ASAP education and rehabilitation programs. *Journal of Safety Research*, 1978, 10, 177–187.

Operation Cork (Producer), and Rogers, G.T. (Director). *Soft Is the Heart of a Child* (Film). Chicago: GTR Productions, 1978.

Popkin, C.L., Lacey, J.H., Li, L.K., Stewart, J.R., and Waller, P.F. An evaluation of North Carolina alcohol and drug education traffic schools. Chapel Hill, North Carolina: UNC Highway Safety Research Center, 1983.

Rapaport, L. The state of crisis: Some theoretical considerations. In H. Parao (Ed.), *Crisis Intervention: Selected Readings*. New York; FSAA, 1965.

Sandler, I., Palmer, S., Holmen, M., and Wynkoop, R. Drinking characteristics of DWIs screened as problem drinkers. *Alcohol Health and Research World*, 1975, Fall, 19–23.

Selzer, M.L. The Michigan Alcohol Screening Test: Reflections on alcoholism screening tests. *Proceedings of the 2nd National DWI Conference*, Rochester Mississippi, May 30–June 1, 1979, Falls Church, Virginia: AAA Foundation for Traffic Safety, 1979.

Strug, E.L. and Hyman, M.M. Social networks of alcoholics. *Journal of Studies on Alcohol*, 1981, 42, 855–884.

U.S. Bureau of the Census, *Statistical Abstract of the United States: 1984*. Washington, D.C., 1983.

U.S. National Institute on Alcohol Abuse and Alcoholism. *Alcohol and Health: Second Special Report to the Congress*. Washington, D.C.: U.S. Government Printing Office, 1974.

U.S. National Institute on Alcohol Abuse and Alcoholism. *Alcohol and Health: Third Special Report to the Congress*. Washington, D.C.: U.S. Government Printing Office, 1979.

Weeber, S. DWI repeaters and non-repeaters: A comparison. *Journal of Alcohol and Drug Education*, 1981, 26, 1–9.

Wegscheider, S. *Another Chance*. Palo Alto, California: Science and Behavior Books, 1981.

Woitiz, J.G. *Adult Children of Alcoholics*. Hollywood, Florida: Health Communications, 1983.

Yoder, R.D. Prearrest behavior of persons convicted of driving while intoxicated. *Journal of Studies on Alcohol*, 1975, 36, 1573–1577.

Yoder, R.D. and Moore, R.A. Characteristics of convicted drunken drivers. *Quarterly Journal of Studies on Alcohol*, 1973, 34, 927–936.

Zylman, R. A critical evaluation of the literature of "Alcohol Involvement" in highway deaths. *Accident Analysis and Prevention*, 1974, 6, 163–204.

The Alteration of Adolescent DUI:
A Macro Level Approach

John S. Wodarski, Ph.D.
Anna P. Fisher

ABSTRACT. The incidence of teenage alcohol abuse and its effect on driving are reviewed. Macro level variables that might be altered to prevent alcohol abuse among teenagers are discussed. The manuscript reviews the following submacro level systems: school and peer environment, home and family, community movements, and business and industry in terms of how they can be employed to prevent alcohol abuse among teenagers. The manuscript concludes with an elucidation of what must be done to influence youths' drinking and subsequent driving behaviors.

Drinking and subsequent driving among teenagers presents a significant social problem in this country. In 1980 alone there were 1,289,443 persons arrested for driving while under the influence of alcohol. Of those, 29,957 were under the age of 18 and 696 were under age 15! And there appears to be a trend toward a progressively worsening situation. Arrests for DUI among the 18 and under age group increased by 236% between 1971 and 1980.

The outcomes of adolescent DUI are deadly. In one account, 43% of the approximately 50,000 persons killed in motor vehicle accidents were correlated with adolescent DUI (Alcohol Health and Research World, 1983). In an address at the NIAAA Alcohol and Drug Education Conference on October 4, 1982, former Health and Human Services Security Director Richard S. Schweider stated that

John S. Wodarski is Director of the Research Center, School of Social Work, University of Georgia, Athens, Georgia 30602.

Anna P. Fisher is affiliated with the Research Center, School of Social Work, University of Georgia, Athens, Georgia 30602.

Preparation of this manuscript was facilitated by a grant from the United States Department of Transportation (DTRS5683-C-00053), the University of Georgia School of Social Work, and the University of Georgia Research Foundation, Inc.

over 10,000 young people die in alcohol-related motor vehicle crashes each year (Allen, 1983, p. 4).

Alcohol use and abuse is widespread among our nation's youth. Based on a 1979 national sample of 2,165 youths, ages 12–17 years, and 2,044 young adults, ages 18–25 years, 70.3% of the youths had used alcohol and 37.2% were current users. In the young adult category, 95.3% had used alcohol and 75.9% were currently using alcohol (U.S. National Institute on Drug Abuse, 1979). Forty percent of these youths live in metropolitan areas where the population is in excess of one million. Another 35% are in metropolitan areas under one million, and 35% live in nonmetropolitan areas. Thus the incidence rate is evenly distributed among urban and rural areas.

Through parents, movies, T.V., and peers, children are impressed with the idea at a very early age that to drive under the influence of alcohol is acceptable. Indeed, it appears that our society has readily accepted drinking and driving as the norm for youth, especially those in their late teens and early adult years.

Adolescents, however, are not ignorant of the risks associated with alcohol use. The Institute for Social Research of the National Institute on Drug Abuse randomly sampled high school seniors in both public and private schools. They were asked the question, "How much do you think people risk harming themselves (physically or in other ways) if they . . . ?" The high school participants, who were all seniors, responded that they perceived "great risk" in alcohol consumption, not only from an occasional drink of beer, wine or liquor (3.8% for 1980) but also for those who "take one to two drinks nearly every day" (20.3% in 1980) to "take five or more drinks once or twice each weekend" (35.9% in 1980) (Johnston, Bachman & O'Malley, 1981, p. 1979).

The statistics bear witness to the gravity of the problem. Youth, along with people of all ages, are dying at an alarming rate on the highways, while at the same time, society is accepting and condoning drinking and driving among teens and others (West, Maxwell, Noble, & Solomon, 1984). Macrosystem changes are called for in order to reorient society to the dangers of its complacency. Drinking and driving teenagers are a problem for all age groups and for the total social system. The individual, his/her peer group, the family (both nuclear and extended), the school, and the community-at-large are all affected by the escapades of just one drinking and driving youth.

Attempts to reverse the trend toward the acceptance of drinking and driving have been characterized by their focus on only certain aspects of the problem. This singular focus has resulted in limited effectiveness of prevention programs (Johnson, 1984; Wodarski, 1984). This manuscript addresses the multiple forces that impact upon the teenage population as well as upon other groups that lead to alcohol consumption and subsequent driving. The aim is to propose means by which to effect macro level change in societal norms and values regarding driving while under the influence.

There are a number of avenues through which change can be made. This mansucript will explore the following subsystems as areas of change: (1) school and peer groups environment, (2) home and family, (3) media, (4) community movements, and (5) business and industry.

School and Peer Group Environment

Youth spend the majority of their lives in the school setting. The school system, therefore, seems to be a natural forum for implementation of change. Educational programs aimed at prevention and early intervention can instill socially acceptable and responsible guidelines for drinking as well as for other problem behaviors.

An awareness of the problem of alcohol use among youth and recognition of ways in which society condones it are steps toward positive change. The schools can be instrumental in educating both the adolescents and their parents. Parents must be knowledgeable of the symptoms of alcohol abuse in adolescents. The usual signs of possible alcohol problems are radical changes in the usual behavioral patterns. "A definite drop in grades, bad conduct and skipping school," are typical according to Pat Schult, senior counselor for the Young Adult Teen on the Alcohol Detoxification Unit at Peachford Hospital, Atlanta, Georgia (Okel, 1984).

Irresponsible alcohol use by teens takes its toll in other ways also. The drinking teen may feel isolated from nondrinking peers. Crime may become a factor to deal with when the adolescent has to steal to maintain drinking habits. There are also developmental issues to be recognized. Adolescents already dealing with stressful changes in their lives may compound the stress with alcohol abuse. They are changing in physical, emotional and sexual ways and must deal with new roles, feelings and identities.

The issue is further compounded by multiple abuse patterns.

Young people frequently use alcohol in combination with other drugs, principally marijuana (Lowman et al., 1982; Turanski, 1983). This combination of alcohol and drugs adds to the difficulty in treating youths and their changing values.

Junior and senior high schools can offer parents an educational and helping network using the school as a meeting place. One school developed such a network through a parent group that initially served in an informational capacity and subsequently as a resource and support group (Turanski, 1983).

Swisher (1976) suggests that programs addressing education and prevention should include "all activities which are *planned* to enrich the personal development of the student . . . including humanistic education, open education, affective education, values clarification, career education and developmental guidance." This is an all-encompassing approach which needs also to be reinforced in the other areas of youths' lives.

The ideal program should have two foci. First, the information transmission approach to provide basic knowledge and awareness, and second, the responsible decision approach that will teach youngsters the basic coping and decision making skills (Schinke & Gilchrist, 1984).

It is important to remember that experimentation with alcohol and peer pressure are related, and that peer pressure will be applied most dramatically in the school. Educators msut aim to make teens more self-confident and less influenced by peer pressure. Globetti (1977) states that "in American society parents and peers are the primary socializing agencies in the onset and emergence of teenage attitudes and behavior regarding alcohol" (p. 167).

Programs must take advantage of peer pressure in a positive manner. To be nonjudgemental and to develop self-esteem in these vulnerable youths are goals of utmost importance and urgency. In program planning there is a need for youth to provide input regarding what they feel are their greatest stresses and programs need to directly address these issues.

Many youths use alcohol as a coping mechanism. School pressures and adolescent growth (both emotional and physical) are all basic life problems. The schools can offer meaningful alternatives to alcohol consumption to help adolescents deal with these stressors. A variety of activities can be offered by schools to provide teenagers reinforcements other than alcohol. These afterschool programs will be successful when they center on youths' interests such as music, fashion, sports and so forth. For example, gyms can be kept open on weekends and during summer months, a small price compared to the effects of alcohol abuse.

The problem in reaching these adolescents comes when they do not see their alcohol use as a problem but as a regular boredom-relieving activity. ''When alcohol-using youth are asked if they see their alcohol use as a problem . . . the most frequently encountered reply is no'' (Turanski, 1983, p. 4). When they do recognize a problem, youth are ill-prepared to seek help. They are more often than not unaware of alcohol prevention and treatment centers. Moreover, they may view these services with mistrust, fear and embarrassment. Another great fear is exposure to both parents and the law. Thus, communication has to occur regarding services that are available. Service providers have to reach out to the youths who are at risk.

To date little emphasis has been placed in educational settings on teenage alcohol use and its subsequent effect on driving (Wodarski, 1984). Two innovative programs with documented success are the ''Sunrise Program'' and the ''Alcohol Education by Teams-Games-Tournaments'' approach.

The Pasadena, California, school district has worked with parents to develop and carry out programs in fifth and sixth grades. These programs use the school as a family support system. Their ''Sunrise Program'' has proven to be ''very successful as both a teaching tool and a means for encouraging community awareness through parental awareness'' (Allen, 1983, p. 6).

''Teams-Games-Tournaments'' (TGT) is another educational approach aimed at teaching youths, through noncompetitive games, to learn self-management skills and facts about alcohol through behavioral analysis (Lenhart & Wodarski, 1983). The goal of the TGT technique is to assist teenagers in making decisions to drink or abstain, how to drink, how often and how much, and to foster the attitude of responsible drinking. The TGT approach is realistic. Its aim is to teach awareness and responsibility and not to proselytize prohibition and abstinence. The uniqueness of TGT is that it capitalizes on peers as teachers to aid in the acquisition of knowledge about alcohol and its effects on driving behavior.

The Family

That ''kids will learn what you tell them about drinking'' is a myth that must be dispelled according to the United States Jaycee's Operation THRESHOLD pamphlet, ''Drinking Myths.'' The fact is that ''your kids will learn what you show them about drinking. If you drink heavily; if you get drunk; the chances are your kids will follow the same example.'' Thus, the mandate is clear that parents must set examples for their children. Young people need positive role models from which to gain their experiences. Data indicate that adolescents are more likely to consume alcohol in a manner similar to that of their parents (Wodarski & Hoffman, 1984) and the parents' drinking behavior is an important influence (Bacon & Jones, 1968).

Drinking is frequently associated with "coming of age" (Pittman & Snyder, 1962), and a driver's license and the availability of alcohol are symbols of adulthood. While forming their new identities, teens need "adult clarification and support in their process of becoming independent" (Lieberman, Caroff & Gottesfeld, 1973).

The family is the "crucial influence on chidren's values and behavior" (Lieberman et al., 1973). In the home, youth can find structure and guidance form loved ones who really care about them. Clear expectations about consumption can be communicated. Younger children are especially vulnerable to pressures and they need a trusting and comfortable place to turn for help in mastering their anxieties and frustrations. The home is the stabilizing influence for youth. It should be the place to turn where alcohol-induced states are not glorified.

Parents must realize that in regard to alcohol and driving they maintain ultimate control. Parents are the resource for the car availability. Mom and Dad have the power to keep the car from abusing adolescents. Parents need to be reinforced that they have the responsibility and right to make decisions that are in the best interests of their children.

Parents may need help in asserting themselves and in coping with difficult situations. Support is available through such mechanisms as Parent Effectiveness Training (PET) classes where parents learn better parenting skills. Through such training, parents learn to set clear expectations about drinking and to enforce consequences when expectations are not met. Moreover, they practice ways to open lines of communication to discuss the use of alcohol and its effects with their teenager.

Media

The media exert a powerful influence on contemporary society. Examples of both positive and negative portrayals of drinking behavior are aired throughout the viewing period. Depending on the programming, the messages are as varied as "drinking is mandated for a good time" and "to be a good friend, do not let your friend drink and drive." Young people "watch television and see the message of what they need and what they should want. 'Tuning in can lead to turning off by turning on'" (Lieberman et al., 1973, p. 110). Also, as Globetti (1977) suggests, "adolescents . . . view alcohol mostly in terms of sociability and in the sense of what it does *for* them rather than *to* them."

The significant impact of daytime and nighttime T.V. "soaps" needs to be evaluated. Such programs as Dallas need parents' interpretation. Excessive consumption as portrayed in these shows is equated with power and success. In reality adolescents must be informed that such consumption more likely impedes success.

The media can likewise exert a powerful positive influence. One of the favorite pastimes of contemporary youth is music. The messages this media conveys must be considered since it is a continual influence. The biggest name in music today is Michael Jackson. Children of all ages have heard him on the radio and have seen him in magazines and newspapers. This young man has had a significant positive influence on youth. His million dollar recording of "Beat It" has been rewritten to address alcohol abuse. Becuase of his commitment to youth, the White House has recognized him with a special plaque and reception hosted by President Reagan (ABC News Announcement, 1984). Positive role models such as Jackson affect the norms of youth and must be capitalized upon. Rather than glorify the consumption of alcohol and its association with adventure and sex, role models can "turn on" teens to more positive outlets.

Community Movements

The ability to influence community norms rests within the community itself. By joining forces and establishing coalitions, standards of acceptance of drinking and driving under the influence of alcohol can be changed (Blansfield, 1984; Gardner, 1983).

Locally sponsored "Soberfests" have provided education and awareness about the impact of irresponsible drinking on society. In some communities, these events are sponsored by a coalition of "business, voluntary organizations, churches and synagogues, universities, tax-supported agencies, hospitals and medical facilities, civic organizations and others who have community 'wellness' and 'a positive, aggressive, innovative approach to health'" as a primary goal. They promote "new norms . . . stay alive; don't drink and drive; get high on life; and, it's OK not to drink" (Athens Community Wellness Council, 1984). Community-wide campaigns promote awareness of behaviors that "add enjoyment and years to life" and are a positive influence on community norms.

Other community organizations, such as the United States Jaycees with the Operation THRESHOLD, have taken steps to offer responsible alternatives to the norms that allow irresponsible drinking and driving under the influence (1983). Mothers Against Drunk Driving (MADD) is a grassroots organization that has succeeded in getting legislation passed for more adequate laws and enforcement. Such groups also provide social support necessary to sustain the work involved in such endeavors (Lindblad, 1983).

Laws and Enforcement

Individual and community involvement and pressure can result in significant social change through governmental legislation and policy. On July 17, 1984, President Reagan signed into law a bill reducing federal highway aid to states that refuse to raise the legal drinking age to 21 by the year 1986. This law also provides extra funding to states that penalize drunken drivers with automatic jail sentences and revoked licenses (Atlanta Journal, July 18, 1984). He changed his original stance on this issue after becoming aware that states that have raised their drinking age have seen a drop in alcohol-related accidents. Government officials, grassroots organizations and private citizens provided the necessary push to get the legislation passed. With this new law comes a clear, though long overdue, message to today's youth—drinking and driving is a problem that requires social action.

Business and Industry

Business and industry have shown concern about irresponsible drinking and driving under the influence of alcohol. They have been spurred to action by data that indicate that productivity is substantially reduced when workers drink excessively (Mayer, 1983). Moreover, they are recognizing that work is a central aspect in many lives and supportive business can foster positive attitudes concerning the consumption of alcohol. Their commitment has been expressed by repeated advertisements in the media. They are reaching a large number of markets through use of printed media, such as advertisements in major magazines. Business sponsored radio and television spots also promote responsible drinking. These spots have been used especially during holiday periods when people of all ages celebrate by irresponsibly using alcohol.

A General Motors advertisement that explains blood alcohol concentrations begins with a disclaimer: "First, you should understand that drinking any amount of alcohol can impair your ability to drive" (General Motors, 1983). The advertisement copy goes on to explain that General Motors has developed a device to test drivers' reflexes and responses before it allows the car to start. The Department of Transportation in California is now testing the device as a deterrent to repeat offenders. General Motors has made other commitments. For example, it set up a program for alcohol abuse in 1972 (Newsweek, August 22, 1983) and it has expanded its Employee Assistance Program to include every General Motors installation in the United States and 12 that are located in Canada.

CONCLUSION

The solution to the problem of alcohol consumption and driving among teens requires an all out effort by those societal forces capable of effecting change. Families, schools, peers, communities, businesses and the media all possess powers to eradicate this social problem. The campaign cannot be waged from only one front, however. Combined, cooperative efforts are essential. The responsibility must be shared for both previous condoning of actions that have perpetuated the problem and for working toward mutual goals and solutions.

REFERENCES

ABC News Announcement, May 10, 1984.
Alcohol Health and Research World, March 3, 1983.
Allen, T.J. The school as a family support system. *The U.S. Journal of Drug and Alcohol Dependence*, 1983, *6* (3), 4.
Athens Community Wellness Council. *Up with wellness*, 1984.
Atlanta Journal, July 18, 1984.

Bacon, M., & Jones, M.B. *Teenage drinking*. New York: Thomas Y. Crowell Company, 1968.

Blansfield, H.N. Drinking and/or driving. *Connecticut Medicine*, 1984, *48* (3), 205.

Gardner, S.E. *Communities: What you can do about drug and alcohol abuse* (DHHS Pub. No. ADM-84-1310). Rockville, MD: National Institute on Drug Abuse, 1983.

General Motors. Customer information from General Motors. *GEO*, July 1983, *5*. (advertisement)

Globetti, G. Teenage drinking. In N.J. Estes and M.E. Heinemann (Eds.), *Alcoholism: Development, consequences and interventions*. St. Louis: C.V. Mosby Company, 1977.

Johnson, N. Research reports: Reducing community alcohol problems. *Alcohol Health and Research World*, 1984, *8* (3), 60–61.

Johnston, L., Bachman, J.B., & O'Malley, P.M. (Eds.), *Highlights from student drug use in America, 1975–1980* (U.S. Department of Health and Human Services, National Institute on Drug Abuse). Washington, DC: U.S. Government Printing Office, 1981, p. 1979.

Lenhart, S.D., & Wodarski, UJ.S. *Alcohol education by the teams-games-tournaments method* (2nd ed.). Minneapolis, MN: Alpha Editions, 1983.

Lieberman, F., Caroff, P., & Gottesfeld, M. *Before addiction: How to help youth*. New York: Behavioral Publications, 1973.

Linblad, R.A. Review of the concerned parent movement in the United States of America. *Bulletin on Narcotics*, 1983, *35* (3), 41–52. (A publication of the National Institute on Drug Abuse.)

Lowman, C., Hubbard, R.L., Rachal, J.V., & Cavanaugh, E.R. Facts for planning: Adolescent marijuana and alcohol use. *Alcohol Health and Research World*, 1982, *6* (3), 69–75.

Mayer, W. Alcohol abuse and alcoholism: The psychologist's role in prevention, research, and treatment. *American Psychologist*, 1983, *38* (10), 1116–1121.

Okel, S. Number one killer of youth. *The Georgia Bulletin*, March 15, 1984, 11.

Pittman, D.J., & Snyder, C.R. (Eds.). *Society, culture and drinking patterns*. Carbondale, IL: Southern Illinois University Press, 1962.

Schinke, S.P., & Gilchrist, L.D. *Life skills counseling with adolescents*. Baltimore: University Park Press, 1984.

Swisher, J.D. An educational policy for school prevention: Rationale and research. *Contemporary Policy Issues*, 1976, *4*, 27–35.

Taking drugs on the job. *Newsweek*, August 22, 1983, 52–60.

Turanski, J.J. Reaching and treating youth with alcohol related problems: A comprehensive approach. *Alcohol Health and Research World*, 1983, *7* (4), 3–9.

U.S. Jaycees. *Drinking myths*. Madison, WI: Wisconsin Clearinghouse.

U.S. National Institute on Drug Abuse. *Statistical abstract of the U.S., National Data Book and Guide to sources* (103rd. ed.). Washington, DC: U.S. Department of Commerce, Bureau of the Census, 1982, 123, tables 195 and 196.

West, L.J., Maxwell, D.S., Noble, E.P., & Solomon, D.H. Alcoholism. *Annals of Internal Medicine*, 1984, *100* (3), 405–416.

Wodarski, J.S., & Hoffman, S.D. Alcohol education for adolescents. *Social Work in Education*, 1984, *6* (2), 69–92.

DUI Offenders and Mental Health Service Providers: A Shotgun Marriage?

Harold Rosenberg, Ph.D.
Bonnie Spiller, M.A.

ABSTRACT. Assessment, education, and rehabilitation programs for DUI offenders are being developed by both private and public community mental health agents to respond to perceived offender needs and perceived sources of revenue. Although such programs may serve an important and beneficial function by reducing recidivism, there are disadvantages to unchecked program development. Questions regarding potential ethical, legal, financial and quality-of-service concerns must be addressed if the proliferation of DUI programs is to be a genuine resource rather than an insufficient and temporary fix for a serious problem.

Perhaps it is not surprising that tougher DUI laws, the raised consciousness of the lay and professional populations, and the increased focus on DUI issues has resulted in an increase in the number of DUI assessment and education programs. This is especially true in jurisdictions where diversion or probation are popular alternatives to traditional criminal penalties.

Most often, these diversion and probation programs for DUI offenders are administered by state, county, or city government agencies who refer the offender to one of a variety of mental health service providers. These include community mental health centers, private, for-profit organizations and private practitioners. Whether this heightened interest and program development is a short-term, flash-in-the-pan or a long-term change in our response to the DUI

Harold Rosenberg is Assistant Professor and Coordinator, Masters Program in Community-Clinical Psychology, at Bradley University, Peoria, IL 61625.
Bonnie Spiller received her M.A. from Bradley University.
We thank Harold Bush for his comments on an earlier draft of this manuscript.

problem, the potential role and power of mental health service providers in this area is increasing.

Perhaps the most important potential outcome of community services involvement would be a decrease in recidivism among program paticipants. Such an effect is difficult to prove, however, because evaluation of the effectiveness of DUI programs is generally rare. This is probably the result of several factors, including non-research attitudes by program developers and the costs of conducting program evaluation.

When it does occur, evaluation can look at both the process of how change occurs and the various outcomes one hopes to achieve (e.g., increased knowledge of basic alcohol information, change in attitude toward driving while intoxicated, cessation of DUI behavior). Unfortunately, evaluation of the latter outcome is hampered by difficulty following-up program participants and assessing whether or not they continue to drive under the influence (not just whether they are re-arrested). Therefore, evaluating claims of program effectiveness is a much more challenging task than developing such programs.

Another possible positive outcome of involvement by mental health personnel is the identification of individuals with alcohol problems. For these persons, driving while intoxicated is one of many maladaptive behaviors that result from an alcohol abuse or dependence problem. Such individuals may be better served in a mental health setting than in the criminal justice system because the criminal penalties these problem drinkers experience are not generally sufficient to change their drinking and DUI behavior.

For example, in his article on accident control, Waller (1967) noted that

> At least half of those involved in drinking accidents are not social drinkers but are people with a long-standing drinking problem [original citations deleted]. Control of drinking and driving in these people would seem to rest more on the identification and treatment of alcoholism than on a heavy fine or suspension of the license, neither of which is therapeutic for the accident problem or for the alcoholism. (p. 96)

Theoretically, mental health personnel are better trained to assess and treat this type of DUI offender and change the underlying cause of the drinking and driving. In contrast, an individual going through the criminal justice system generally would not receive an adequate assessment or opportunity to change the underlying cause of the DUI problem.

Although these advantages and others would seem to favor increasing the role of community mental health resources in diversion and probation, there are some potential disadvantages that must be addressed. For example, requiring DUI offenders, as part of their diversion or probation, to undergo an evaluation (and treatment if an alcohol disorder is present) assumes several things. First, it assumes that we can reliably and accurately recognize an alcohol problem when one is actually present and, just as important, that we recognize when one is not present. Such a state of diagnostic reliability and accuracy has not been established in this population of evaluators.

For example, as part of a recent study of diagnostic practices (Spiller, 1984), DUI evaluators registered by the state of Illinois were asked to give their diagnostic impression of an individual described in a case report. One of the reports contained a variety of background information about a fictitious client, including his recent arrest for a second DUI. Purposefully excluded were signs of alcohol abuse or dependence according to DSM-III (APA, 1980). Responses of subjects ranged from diagnostic statements indicating no problem (e.g., "no alcohol problem" and "no significant chemical problem") to those indicating uncertainty about the presence of a problem (e.g., "a potential drinking problem," "rule out alcoholism" and "borderline probability of dependence") to those indicating a definite diagnosis of an alcohol problem (e.g., "DSM-III 305.02 Alcohol abuse, episodic," "early to middle stage alcoholism," and "problematic alcohol abuser with an intermittent appetite characterized by periodic episodes in which loss of control is indicated . . . "). Some subjects indicated that there was not enough information to make a diagnostic statement.

These subjects used different criteria to evaluate the case report, including those of DSM-III, the National Council on Alcoholism, and personal experience. Unfortunately, these inconsistent (and invalid) diagnostic practices can lead to a serious problem—individuals who have been arrested for one or more DUIs, but who do not have an alcohol disorder, may be labeled with an alcohol or other diagnosis that is unwarranted but stigmatizing.

The evaluation problem is, of course, a prelude to a second and equally vexing problem. Even if we could reliably and accurately identify individuals with an alcohol problem, do we have the techniques to consistently and effectively treat such problems? Boasting and propaganda aside, it appears that *no* method of alcohol treatment (including the ubiquitous A.A.) is consistently effective.

For example, Ditman and his colleagues (1967) conducted a controlled study in which "chronic drunk offenders" were randomly assigned to either no treatment, alcohol clinic, or A.A. as a condition of a one-year probation. The results were that over two-thirds of the offenders sent to A.A. and the clinic were rearrested during the follow-up. The recidivism rates of the three groups were not significantly different, but it is interesting that 44% of the no-treatment group were *not* rearrested compared to only one-third of the treated groups. This is not to say that alcohol education and rehabilitation are never efficacious, only that we should not assume that the mental health system is a panacea for those DUI offenders with an alcohol disorder.

Another issue that arises as DUI services become popular is the potentially large amount of money to be made by charging assessment and program fees. This income is attractive not only to financially strapped government bodies, but also to financially strapped mental health centers and private practitioners. Unfortunately, some of these agencies and individuals are more interested in dollars than quality of assessment and education services.

The amount of money paid by the participants in these programs can vary extensively. This may lead to differential financial burdens on participants merely as a result of their geographical location or the program to which they are referred. For example, when we reviewed the June 1983 list of the certified DUI assessment and program resources in the state of Illinois, we found that the average fee for an alcohol assessment was $56, but the range was from nothing to over $200. Similarly, although the average program fee was almost $120, fees ranged from almost nothing to almost $500.

The number of hours of required attendance and the content of the programs may vary as well. Our review found that, although the average program consists of almost 11 1/2 hours of instruction, program lengths range from 7 hours to 44 hours. Perhaps not surprisingly, as the program length increases, so does the program fee, although the correlation is not high ($r = .44$).

In addition, the duration of an education program may be unrelated to the individual attention received by a participant. Although the Illinois list did not contain any overall data on class size, we have observed that DUI program classes may range from 10 persons to over 40 class members. Larger class sizes and the nature of the classroom setting tends to limit recognition of and attention to individual differences and individual needs. Yet these diversion and probation programs are supposed to be better equipped to meet these individual needs compared to the criminal justice system.

We are also concerned about an ethical problem that can arise when an agency or practitioner offers a combination of assessment, education, and rehabilitation services for DUI offenders. For example, in Illinois, DUI convicts must produce evidence they do not have a serious drinking problem before their licenses are reinstated. They are required to have an alcohol evaluation, and treatment if necessary.

Mental health workers may find themselves in a conflict of interest position if they have the authority to require additional therapy or education after an individual's program participation or alcohol assessment. The problem is that the practitioner or agency who recommends further rehabilitation may be the one who benefits directly from such a recommendation—perhaps without judicial oversight or client opportunity for appeal. If such a conflict of interest is recognized by the evaluator, this individual should make referrals to other community service providers (*without* a quid pro quo agreement), even when he or she is one who can provide that service.

An additional conflict of interest may arise if the mental health worker is not clear, either with himself or the service recipients, about which of several parties is the client. For example, is the DUI offender the client, who has the right of confidentiality and for whom the professional is an advocate? Is the referring judge or probation department the client, who has the right to all information gathered during assessment and/or rehabilitation? Or, is society the client, who should be protected from the offender's potential future dangerousness?

The outcome for the offender, the criminal justice system agents, and society will be different depending upon which role the mental health worker assumes. A genuine balancing of these conflicting interests is likely to be difficult to achieve and perhaps just as likely to lead to abuse of the offender's rights and society's needs. At the very least, an evaluator, instructor, or therapist must explicitly inform all parties concerned where his or her loyalties lie.

The final issue we raise concerns the transfer of the DUI offender from the criminal justice system to the mental health system. This may enable the person to escape or decrease legal punishment. Also, the offender may lose due process protections provided by the criminal justice system. We wonder if treatment of a criminal behavior as if it were a mental disorder is an inappropriate use of the mental health system to do the job of the criminal justice system.

REFERENCES

American Psychiatric Association (1980). *Diagnostic and statistical manual of mental disorders* (3rd ed.). Washington, DC: Author.
Dittman, K.S., Crawford, G.G., Forgy, E.W., Moskowitz, H., & MacAndrew, C. (1967). A controlled experiment on the use of court probation for drunk arrests. *American Journal of Psychiatry, 124*, 160–163.
Spiller, B. (1984). *A survey of the diagnostic practices of DUI evaluators.* Unpublished master's thesis, Bradley University, Peoria, IL.
Waller, J.A. (1967). Control of accidents in rural areas. *Journal of the American Medical Association, 201*, 94–98.

The Longwood Treatment Center: A Residential Program for Multiple O.U.I. Offenders

Stephen K. Valle, Sc.D., C.A.C., F.A.C.A.T.A.
Tess Kerns, M.Ed., C.A.C.
Allen W. Gaskell, M.S., C.A.C.

Providing effective treatment for multiple O.U.I. offenders represents one of the most difficult challenges for treatment professionals. Multiple offenders have a history of resistance to therapeutic intervention and, until recently, have represented a small segment of the patient population usually seen in treatment facilities. Public pressure for increased enforcement of drunk driving laws and more severe penalties for drivers who repeatedly drive while under the influence of alcohol has changed this pattern. These individuals are identified as needing treatment; however, they often do not appear in treatment facilities. Rather, they are "treated" in the correctional systems because of their repeated offenses. This has often resulted in an increased burden upon an already overcrowded correctional system as more and more people are receiving mandatory sentences. These individuals usually have been in treatment previously and also have attended one or more alcohol safety education programs.

Historically, treatment professionals have responded to this special population by designing out-patient programs to treat multiple offenders; however, out-patient educational and treatment programs developed to address the problem of drunk drivers in general, and multiple offenders in particular, have yielded conflicting evidence concerning the effectiveness of out-patient programs in reducing recidivism (Brown, 1980; Cameron, 1979; Ellingsted and Springer, 1976; Zador, 1976). While the literature reports a proliferation of out-patient models and programs designed to address the multiple offender, we were unable to identify a treatment facility reported in the literature which exclusively addressed the multiple offender on an inpatient residential basis.

Recognizing that 25% of commitments to local houses of correction in Massachusetts were multiple O.U.I. offenders, the Massachusetts Department of Corrections, in cooperation with the Governor's office and the Division of Alcoholism, established a separate minimum security facility, the Longwood Treatment Center, designed specifically for treatment of the multiple O.U.I. offender. Recognizing that specific expertise was needed to plan, implement, and evaluate such a unique treatment facility, the Department of Corrections requested proposals from providers for the design and management of treatment for this new and innovative program. The program design and structure of the Longwood Treatment Center is described below.

PROGRAM STRUCTURE

The Longwood Treatment Center is a 125 bed inpatient, minimum security facility operated by the Massachusetts Department of Corrections. The treatment program, designed and managed by Valle Associates, Inc., provides a comprehensive range of services within the structure of a minimum security correctional setting. An initial screening assessment is conducted to determine appropriateness for treatment by the Department of Corrections staff. After inmates are determined to be appropriate for treatment, they enter the program which has three phases. Programs are individualized for inmates, depending upon the length of the inmate's sentence and their progress in attaining the goals and objectives established in their individualized treatment plan.

Initial Screening Assessment

The screening of inmates for participation in the treatment program is done on the basis of their motivation and willingness to participate in the treatment program at Longwood. Screenings are conducted by the Department of Corrections staff at the county houses of correction whee an inmate is currently serving a jail sentence for multiple drunk driving offenses. Eligibility requires that inmates have committed only alcohol-related crimes and are already serving time. The sentences vary from two months to one year or more. These sentences are often amended due to time off for good behavior or parole, but on the average the sentences (actual time served) range from one month to one year within the Longwood program.

PHASE I

Phase I consists of an orientation to the facility, a comprehensive evaluation, educational lectures and treatment sessions.

The initial orientation is performed by the Department of Corrections staff who introduce inmates to the facility and its staff, and familiarize inmates with departmental rules and regulations. During this process, inmates are assigned a code number, are photographed, and are assigned a Department of Corrections counselor. This counselor serves as a link between the treatment staff and the Department of Corrections.

Following the initial orientation, the Department of Corrections staff conduct a complete medical screening and evaluation to rule out the need for medical detoxification or the existence of any medical condition which requires medical intervention.

Inmates are then introduced to the Valle Associates treatment staff, familiarized with the treatment program, and briefed on their rights and responsibilities. They are then given a battery of assessment instruments which are utilized in developing the inmates' individualized treatment plans. This assessment process results in a problem list and an initial treatment plan that provides the basis for the first 10 to 14 days of treatment. In order to coordinate the inmates' treatment process, a Classification Board hearing is held on all inmates. The Board consists of representatives from the Department of Corrections' counseling, security and administrative staffs, and representatives from the Valle Associates treatment staff.

Following the orientation and evaluation process described above, the inmates are placed in groups of 10 to 12 members. There is an attempt to match individuals with therapists whose styles are most conducive for their treatment process. Treatment plans are written and updated at least twice during the first four week segment. Classification Board meetings are also conducted to review client progress.

The treatment components of Phase I are:

1. Educational Lecture, 2 one-half-hour segments per day

2. Small Group Therapy, 2 hours per day
3. Special Focus Groups, 1 session per week
4. Outside Lecturers (AA, Al-Anon, MADD, NA, clergy)
5. Family and Friends Meetings, 2 times per week.

During the four to five weeks in which inmates are involved in the treatment process of Phase I, there are a series of educational lectures on topics such as the Disease Process, Family Dynamics, Communication Skills, Denial, and Cross Addiction. The lecture series is designed to be on a 30-day rotation process where inmates may enter at any point in the process.

In addition to the educational lectures, there are two daily one-hour group therapy sessions. Inmates are assigned to a group designed to maintain consistency and continuity by having the same participants and group leader each day. The groups are run on a traditional interactional group process format to address specific areas of the inmates' treatment plan.

Each client is assessed for appropriateness for attending a special focus group. These groups are directed by a therapist and focus on special problems inherent with alcohol dependence. The groups are: Women's Issues, Adult Children of Alcoholic Parents, Relapse Prevention, and the Twelves Steps of Alcoholics Anonymous. These special focus groups enable the client to interact with other members of the treatment team and to work on special issues which may not be adequately dealt with in lecture or group therapy. They also permit the client to interact with the other inmates other than those in his/her group therapy.

There is an attempt to broaden the inmates' experience at Longwood through incorporating Alcoholics Anonymous, Al-Anon, Mothers Against Drunk Driving, and Narcotic Anonymous into the Therapeutic regimen. The response to these special groups has been excellent. Inmates often feel a sense of isolation and loneliness while incarcerated, but this is somewhat balanced by the outside groups who come in voluntarily in an effort to provide emotional support. There has been a particularly good response from A.A., which has responded with volunteers, many of whom have had previous experience with prison due to their own alcohol-related problems. The rationale behind this kind of exposure is to prepare the inmate for the kind of support services available upon release.

The role of spirituality in recovery from alcoholism is also considered to be an important treatment concern. The Longwood

DOC has developed a very loyal group of clergy who serve as contacts with their churches. There is a Church service for Catholics on Fridays and for Protestants on Saturdays and Sundays, and Valle Associates offers an alternative activity on Spirituality and Alcoholism on Fridays for any who wish to participate. This involves a series on the spiritual aspect of recovery and disease process of alcoholism. Further development of this aspect of the program is expected during the next year.

Special attention is given to the role of families in supporting abstinence or enabling the inmates' continued drinking. Family and Friends meetings are held on Thursday nights and Saturday afternoons in order to provide support and treatment for the family member. Because the focus of the treatment is on the inmate and not the family, we are able to provide only basic education and a forum for questions and answers. We hope to expand this program over the next year.

Once the goals and objectives of Phase I have been completed, clients must pass a written and oral battery of "tests" on the following areas: the disease concept of alcoholism; communication skills; the family and alcoholism; cross addiction. Successful completion of these tests is necessary to become eligible for continuation in the program onto Phase II, and some clients are required to repeat classes within Phase I before continuing the treatment process. The written examination is an attempt to evaluate the clients' cognitive abilities and the extent of memory process impairment still in existence. The "oral" portion is an attempt to validate the client's progress in treatment and to assess attitude and appropriateness for further treatment.

The focus in Phase I is on the inmates themselves and on their gaining understanding of the problem which put them in jail in the first place—alcohol. The program in Phase I is structured on helping the inmates take responsibility for their actions and on diffusing unhealthy anger and resentment against society or the criminal justice system.

PHASE II

Inmates who are determined to be ready to enter the Phase II aspect of the program must have at least four weeks left in their sentence and possess a basic understanding of the topics previously mentioned.

Phase II is a much less structured program than Phase I and is designed to foster self-reliance and dependence on one's self instead of the therapy team. There is mandatory journal writing, daily lectures and group therapy. There are also daily directed study assignments in leisure skills and personal growth and development. The focus of this Phase of treatment is on communication skills, problem solving skills, and appropriate expression of feelings which have previously immobilized the inmate or produced uncontrolled drinking.

Group therapy to explore new techniques for communicating and coping is enhanced through video and other media. These skills are modeled and practiced in group, and inmates continue to use them outside of therapy until they can successfully demonstrate these new skills in progressively more stressful environments.

PHASE III

Once the inmate has successfully completed Phase II, and is eligible for work-release status, he/she enters Phase III of the treatment program. On work release, the inmate becomes reclassified from "minimum security" to "pre-release" and is able to work outside the facility. A special treatment component is currently being created for these inmates in order to continue the treatment process in a real life situation. In order to be eligible for work release, the inmate must be recommended for a reduction in security status by a five-member Classification Board.

Work release inmates in Phase III must adhere to the following program requirements:

1. attendance at 3 AA meetings outside the institution weekly
2. attendance at weekly relaxation therapy group
3. attendance at weekly group therapy
4. attendance at weekly structured 12 step meetngs
5. adherence to a directed study program designed for each inmate.

The goal of this phase is to equip the inmates with the necessary skills for living drug and alcohol free.

INDICATIONS FOR TREATMENT PERSONNEL

The Longwood Treatment Program represents a unique challenge to alcoholism treatment professionals. Traditional alcoholism treatment services are being applied in a very untraditional setting—the correctional system. And this system has a significant impact upon commonly held beliefs and approaches to treatment.

It is often difficult, though very important, for treatment personnel to remember that their clients are, in fact, inmates who have committed a crime against society. While alcoholism treatment personnel must educate and treat clients regarding their alcoholism, they must also work closely with correctional personnel whose primary responsibility is to see that inmates are rehabilitated while serving out their prison sentence.

Because of the different focus of alcoholism treatment and correctional personnel, it is important that these staffs work closely together to attain the ultimate goal of returning inmates to society with the acknowledgement that they committed a crime for which they were responsible to society, as well as educating and treating inmates about the disease from which they suffer. Each staff can learn and benefit from the unique skills that each possess to deal concurrently with the complex disease of alcoholism and the behavioral challenges presented by this population.

Avoiding staff splitting is a constant challenge that both staffs need to pay particular attention to given the nature of the client population and the length of time residents are in treatment. Both staffs are working on devising strategies to coordinate treatment to insure that there is continuity between the two systems.

A crucial issue for treatment professionals is the effect treatment efforts are having on client outcome. Research designed to measure the impact of the program on a variety of client, public safety, recidivism, and personal, family and social functioning outcome indices is in the process of being developed and will provide additional input for program design as data is received.

The Longwood Treatment Center represents an innovative approach to treating the multiple O.U.I. offender as it combines the resources of alcoholism treatment professionals with those of correctional professionals. While only in its infancy, the program represents a commitment and partnership that is both challenging and rewarding.

REFERENCES

Brown, R.A. Conventional education and controlled drinking education courses with convicted drunken drivers. *Behavior Therapy*, 632–642, *11*, 1980.

Cameron, Tracy et al. *Alcohol, Casualties and Crimes*. Alcohol and Traffic, Chapter 3. Social Research Group, School of Public Health, University of California, Berkeley, CA, 1978.

Ellingstad, Vernon S., and Springer, Timothy J. Program Evaluation of ASAP Diagnosis, Referral and Rehabilitation Efforts. Analysis ASAP Rehabilitation Countermeasures Effectiveness, Volume III. Final Report Prepared for U.S. Department of Transportation, 1976.

Zador, P. Statistical Evaluation of the Effectiveness of Alcohol Safety Action Projects. *Accident Analysis & Prevention*, 51–59, *8*, 1976.